Planning Your Business in the 'Horse as Healer/Teacher' Professions

ARIANA STROZZI

PLANNING YOUR BUSINESS IN THE 'HORSE AS HEALER/TEACHER' PROFESSIONS

INTRODUCTION

First of all, welcome to this exciting new field of incorporating horses into human development growth and learning. In this book, I will refer to this rapidly developing field as Equine Guided Education (EGE). I hope that even if you call your work by another acronym that this book will still be useful for you. I have been fortunate to discover this work in the late 1980's and have watched it blossom over the years. Interacting with horses is a profound and unique way to learn about the self, review life, get in touch with one's passion and life purpose as well as a way to develop new skills and insights. Horses are magical and mysterious, intuitive and sensate, serious and playful, rigorous and patient. I truly believe that EGE is the missing piece to our historic models of education and learning.

Perhaps one hundred years ago, learning from horses was natural since they graced our daily lives in work, transportation, city streets and as archetypal creatures of mythology. Choosing to get involved in EGE will prove to be both exciting and challenging. So prepare yourself for a journey. Allow yourself to become a life-long learner–one who continues to open her consciousness to new and nontraditional perspectives. Become a student of the horse and those who have graced this path before you. It's ok to not know everything. In fact, it is your willingness to let go of what you know that will allow you to walk into this work with a childlike curiosity and allow it to become the work of art that it is meant to be.

Having just said to let go of what you know, many of you may still feel like you need to be clear on how to proceed. Therefore, I am offering this book as a map to follow and a resource for specific topics. Having been a professional coach to thousands of people from various walks of life and a successful entrepreneur, I am offering not only what I have learned, but practices that have proven extremely useful to me as a business owner and to my clients. Some of the chapters in this book might not be relevant for you, so skip to the chapters that are of particular interest. You do not need to read this book sequentially.

Some of the topics discussed in this book regarding various associations are current through the beginning of 2009. As this industry continues to grow and change rapidly some of the information in the chapter, "What to Call What You Do," may change over time. Please note that I will refer to the 'Horse as Healer/Teacher' professions as EGE (Equine Guided Education) in this book for simplicity. This is not meant to exclude other popular acronyms. If you are or plan to refer to your professional title by some other acronym such as EAP/EAL or EFL/EFP, then mentally replace my reference of EGE with your preferred acronym.

While embarking in this work is exciting, it can also be challenging. It requires rigor and commitment. It requires leadership to create a successful business as discussed in the chapter, "Successful Skill Sets of a Business Owner." It requires you to be all of who you're meant to be. It takes time, like any new venture does. It demands skill, finesse and creativity. Its bounty is in your imagination, passing through your dreams, calling you to awaken to another–far more interesting–realm of consciousness. Trust yourself.

The most important factor in learning this work is that you become a student of the horse, of people, of elders, of life, of land and nature. Educate yourself in this field before you expose your students and clients to it. EGE is important and complex. It requires not only equine skill, but human development skill as well. Even for those folks who have extensive competency in both areas, the EGE process still requires additional training, education and practice. It is not as simple as just putting your and human experience together and bringing people out to experience your great idea.

EGE is an unpredictable process that defies your best made plans and can become unexpectedly dangerous due to the simple fact that horses are unpredictable, large, quickly moving animals with minds of their own that respond to the complex inner emotional and psychological landscape of the humans in their close proximity. And, no matter how skilled you are, you cannot ever presuppose to know or understand for yourself what another person is thinking deep inside of their subconscious. And until you have witnessed this work over an extensive period of time, you may not fully understand what you are taking on.

So a word of advice: Study, learn, and practice with the mentoring of a teacher and/or program that specializes in teaching professionals. Most importantly, find a teacher whose competency and stylistic approach you respect. Just because you may be the most awesome amazing coach, does not make you a great EGE person overnight. Be patient. Where there is a will, there is a way. And fortunately for you, there are now resources out there for you to learn from experienced practioners and become a member of this evolving discourse. Remember life (and your life's work) is a path to follow, not an end point: a destination to arrive at. Enjoy the path, remember to breathe and take time to smell the flowers.

STEPPING OUT OF HORSEMANSHIP
AS WE HAVE KNOWN IT

(Excerpted from an article I wrote for a traditional horsemanship magazine)

If I were to say in a nutshell what I have learned from horses it would be that, "Horses make decisions based on how they FEEL, not on what they THINK." Like wild animals, they rely on their intuition–pre-cognitive, sensate feelings–when relating to humans, other animals and their surroundings. When a horseperson opens their mind to this concept, a whole new way of being with horses becomes possible. Think about how different our lives could be if we could learn to stop thinking so much about how we are doing and what other people think of us and trust that we already know what is going on without having to think so hard.

Horses listen and respond to what is happening on the inside of a person first. They can sense when a person is afraid, timid, angry, calm, balanced. They want to know if we really care about what we are asking of them, if we are inspired by the possibility of oneness. Their ability to sense 'who we are behind our tools' is_ their primary source of communication. The various tools and techniques that exist in the horse world are secondary and tertiary forms of communication that often rely on conditioning the horse into a specific type of performance though subordination.

Every horseperson has heard the phrase, "You need to be the leader of the horse." But what does this really mean? Does it mean to dominate, to control, to be the 'boss'? In Intuitive Horsemanship™ I like to reframe the concept of being the leader of the horse to mean being the 'guide' who sets the direction and purpose of what horse and rider are doing together and, in turn, the horse is the 'guide' of the emotional-spiritual realm. This reframing of the horse-human roles allows the horse to be the sensate being that it is, always giving us feedback when we are effective and when we are not. I'm sure every horse person in the world has had their share of 'humble pie' handed to them by a horse. The horse will always tell us when we are not aligned mentally/physically/spiritually. If we can learn to respect this mutual, reciprocal relationship with horses, we can find that Harmony that we all seek.

Imagine the horsewoman who comes out to the barn after a hard day's work. She's still uptight from the stress of her day. Her face is pinched, her breath short, her jaw clenched. Her horse fidgets and tosses his head while tied. She grooms the horse faster, still not breathing. He fidgets more. After saddling her restless horse, she enters the arena only to have him wiggle and prance around her while she is trying to mount. She still doesn't notice that he is just mirroring her mood. She tightens her jaw more. "Damn horse," she whispers. He flares his nostrils, "I'm just reflecting how you are feeling," he whispers.

She is so frustrated she wants to scream, but then she remembers this new concept that she learned–her horse's attitude is a reflection of her attitude. She stops what she is doing. Takes several deep breaths, relaxes her jaw, empties her mind by feeling her feet on the ground and the breeze on her face. After several minutes she feels centered again and she mounts her horse, who is now standing quietly beside her. She didn't need any tools or fancy techniques to quiet her horse; she just needed to quiet herself. She focused on how she was 'feeling', not on what she was 'thinking'. She got out of her mind's agenda to ride the horse. She re-connected to her desire to meet the horse as a partner, not a dominator. Basically, she had allowed herself to become a student of the horse. This shifting of perspective, from dominator to partner, allows a whole new world to open up not only in traditional horsemanship models, but also in the new field of Equine Guided Education (EGE).

Equine Guided Education takes this concept one step further by allowing the horse to do what it is already doing–listening to what is happening on the inside of a person. Stepping out of traditional horsemanship models in which the horse has to be controlled, the EGE process focuses on allowing the horse to reflect how the person is 'being' in the world distinct from how they think they are being. The horse's sensate wisdom and its insistence on honest communication, provides profound and unique insights into how the person is dealing with other areas of their personal and professional life.

Ariana Strozzi

Another gift that horses bring to human learning methods is their willingness of spirit, openhearted patience and non-judgmental presence. The fact that horses do not judge us as 'good' or 'bad' people allows humans to break away from historic, cultural and familial conclusions that are rife with moral undertones. In order to truly create a space for learning about the self–to re-discover who we are at our core; to reconnect to our spiritual values and beliefs about life, place and purpose; to follow our destiny; to find our calling; to heal what has been broken–a non-judgmental, inquisitive approach is necessary. Why? Because our judgments about 'who we are' and 'who we are not' (as told to us by other humans or self-created) inhibit significant learning, growth and change. Many of these stories about the self are actually inaccurate, outdated and largely unexamined or even unconscious. Horses help us uncover these self-limiting judgments and create new, more optimistic interpretations.

The horse in an EGE process has an uncanny ability to get through our conscious barriers and listen to our core longing or life force. In addition, people will accept the horse's insights/reflections in a way that they often will not or cannot hear from another human being. In effect, horses help to reveal core issues, outdated patterns of thought and behavior dramatically faster, more accurately and deeper than just talking therapy or coaching. The horse bypasses our intellectual games and goes right to the heart of the matter. Literally. In fact, the conversation about Heart Energy is a whole topic in and of itself that is discussed in greater detail in the EGE manual.

SHIFTING PARADIGMS FROM HORSEMANSHIP TO 'HORSE AS HEALER/TEACHER'

EGEA research indicates that 'Horse as Healer/Teacher' began surfacing right around 1990. Perhaps there was a time before witches were burned at the stake that it existed, we may never know. I believe that many of the greatest horsewomen and men knew it, but kept it to themselves, or left it in the arena when they were done working with horses for the day. Until the late 1980's it was largely a secret conversation. Individual experiences of healing and learning from horses were too scandalous to mention publicly.

Sally Swift's book, *"Centered Riding"*, published in 1985 was one of the first books to expose the concept that horsemanship was not about dominating and controlling horses, but rather a discipline of the self. Written for the equestrian she brought forward the concept that riding horses effectively had something more to do with how the rider was 'being' distinct from the tools or techniques he/she was performing.

Tom Dorrance began to articulate the same notion in his book, *"True Unity"* published in 1987:

> *"There is so much variation in the human individual that the approach has to be a little different in order to fit each person. They might come out with the same results as someone else, but if everyone tried to take the same approach, there wouldn't be too many of them coming out with the same solution. That's another thing I think is important to emphasize—this is an individual process. I tell people that over and over when they are trying to get something worked out. I say, ' all I can do is try to help.' It has to come right out of the inside of the individual. There is no other way I know of that they can get it. People tend to say, "that's a little deep, I know what you are saying but I don't understand it...The true unity and willing communication between the horse and me is not something that can be handed to someone. It has to be learned. It has to come from the inside of a person and the inside of a horse. Mind, body and spirit."*

Ray Hunt, one of Tom's best students wrote:

> *"My goal with the horse is not to beat it, it's to win within myself. To do the best job I can do and tomorrow try to do better. You will be working on yourself to accomplish this, not on your horse...It's the confidence you give your horse and the understanding; the purpose and meaning behind what you ask him to do that is going to make the big difference."*

These horsemen, teaching traditional horsemanship in a natural way, began to articulate some of the universal principles behind

Ariana Strozzi

'Horse as Healer/Teacher', but I don't think they took their wisdom out of the arena. By this I mean, they did not step out of the horsemanship model to really relate the profoundness–the broader applications–of these concepts to human development. They may have seen and understood the 'Horse as Healer/Teacher', but they chose to keep it within the horsemanship model.

Subsequent generations of horsemen and women began to expand on these earlier teachings and began to explore how the practices they had with their horses could apply to other areas of their life. Some of the principles in natural styles of horsemanship maintain the same beliefs towards horses as EGE:

- Observe, remember, and compare
- The slower you do it, the quicker you find it
- Feel what the horse is feeling
- Do less and get more
- The horse is never wrong

'Horse as Healer/Teacher' takes these concepts several steps further. What we have learned since the late 1980's is that a person can focus on personal or professional issues while they are interacting with horses (rather than focusing on horsemanship itself) and receive dramatic, unique, profound and concise feedback that pertain to their real life. Uncanny, magical, mysterious? Yes to all. Beyond Cartesian understanding? Yes. Yet the information gained is far more useful and impactful than traditional talking therapy or coaching models.

WHAT DO I MEAN BY 'HORSE AS HEALER/TEACHER'?

I will discuss this question by defining what Equine Guided Education, as I believe that it defines all of the work before one begins to specialize with a specific group of people and issues. The Equine Guided Educator creates an experiential, supportive learning environment for participants to learn about themselves, heal what has been broken, and re-connect to what has heart and meaning through interactive experiences with horses. He/she allows the horse to 'guide' the process of exploration, learning, reflection. He/she combines the process of kinesthetic learning and cognitive reflection in relation to the student's/client's mental, physical, spiritual, emotional and social well-being. Through the process of evaluating an individual's current patterns of behavior, perceptions, and performance, the Equine Guided Educator encourages the student/client towards a healthy self-image and supports the exploration of new practices for achieving personal and/or professional goals.

The Equine Guided Educator guides his/her students/clients through a learning process that is centered on their ambitions and goals for the future. He/she assists his/her students/clients in refining their gifts and creating environments in which they can thrive. He/she facilitates the student's/client's growth and learning through experiential exercises with horses. The horse, in this process, literally 'guides' the student/client and the educator by revealing inner states of mind and physical energetic states of presence. The noun "guide" means "someone who can find paths through unexplored territory." The Equine Guided Educator as "Educator" cultivates the integration of mind/body/spirit through experiential learning practices.

The combination of the Educator and the Equine Guide offers unique, impactful, experiential exercises geared towards developing people's self knowledge and self-responsibility. Some common learning schemas include:

- Identifying and developing the student/client ambitions and aspirations
- Developing the ability to stay focused on goals and projects
- Enhancing communication and negotiation skills
- Encouraging self confidence and self-esteem
- Assisting the process of developing trust with oneself and others
- Learning how to listen to and respect one's intuition and sixth sense
- Building effective relationship and interactive practices

Uncovering old stories and behaviors that are no longer effective

 Developing new stories and behaviors relevant to goals and objectives

The Equine Guided Educator understands how to allow the horse to reflect each student's/client's unique strategies and presentations in such a way that the student/client can receive this often intense feedback in a supportive process. Leveraging the process of 'learning by doing' (experiential) integrated with the horse's natural wisdom and healing presence assists the Educator in encouraging the student/client to accept responsibility for their own learning and behavior.

The word "Experience" is defined as the state or extent of being engaged in a particular study or work; developing knowledge, skill or technique resulting from experience; the sum total of the conscious events which compose an individual life as observed facts and events in contrast with what is supplied by thought. Effective learning occurs when the student/client engages in some activity, reflects upon the activity, derives useful insight from the analysis, and incorporates the result through a change in understanding and/or behavior. As Lao Tzu once quoted, "You cannot learn from a good book, because a book will not tell you what you do not want to hear."

WHAT TO CALL WHAT YOU DO?

EGE, EFP, EAP, AND THE ACRONYM DELUGE

One cannot enter this field without experiencing at least mild confusion about where to start. What do all these different acronyms mean? Which one should I align with? In the next few paragraphs I will attempt to offer some clarifications from my perspective. My attempt is an attempt at best. Even as I have been writing this book, acronyms and what they mean to whom, keep changing. I do not intend to offend anyone in my interpretation. My intention is to offer you some ways to think about the acronym deluge and to hopefully, find the clarity you need to determine the acronym you would like to use.

As of winter 2008, the Equine Guided Education Association (EGEA) counted over forty-four acronyms currently in use. See Appendix D for a partial list. Many of the acronyms are spin offs of the three original acronyms that first came to form in the pioneering days of the 1990s: EGE (Equine Guided Education), EAP (Equine Assisted Psychotherapy) and EFP (Equine Facilitated Psychotherapy). These three acronyms are the most widely recognized and have been around the longest. They can be sourced back to a point of origin and are connected to specific associations.

EGE is supported by EGEA (Equine Guided Education Association), EFP is supported by EFMHA (Equine Facilitated Mental Health Association), and EAP is supported by EAGALA (Equine Assisted Growth and Learning Association). They each have a clear definition of meaning and interpretation. They have market recognition with insurance companies and other professional institutions. Each acronym stays the same when one describes 'what they do' and 'who they are'. For example, an Equine Guided Educator (EGE) does Equine Guided Education (EGE); the acronym stays the same in labeling what they do and what they offer. An Equine Assisted Psychotherapist (EAP) does

Equine Assisted Psychotherapy (EAP). Whereas a professional offering Equine Assisted Learning (EAL) is a "?", I am not sure.

Offshoots of EAL include HAL (horse assisted learning), EAC (equine assisted coaching), EALC (equine assisted learning and coaching), EAEL (equine assisted experiential learning), HAC (horse assisted coaching) and HAE (horse assisted education). Offshoots of EFP include, EFL (equine facilitated learning), EELC (equine experiential learning and coaching), EEL (equine experiential learning), and EFEL (equine facilitated experiential learning). Even EGE is being extrapolated into EGL (equine guided learning), HGL (horse guided learning), EGC (equine guided coaching), etc.

The sad part of the story is that these forty plus acronyms currently in use to describe this work are diluting our ability to create a truly consistent, reliable industry that the public can readily understand and that other professionals deem credible.

What are these acronyms attempting to accomplish? Why has there been an explosion of additional acronyms attempting to define this profession? Is the acronym deluge a branding issue? Is it better for professionals to brand their professional 'identity' rather than their professional 'offer'? Is it a trade issue? Without a trade name for this growing industry how do we define or label ourselves? Is it causing problems in terms of our credibility and recognition by other professionals and the insurance industry? These are all relevant questions and subject of much debate around many a dinner table that I have been present to over the last several years.

Let me illustrate our current dilemma by offering a recent discussion with a new member of EGEA. This new member is a perfect example of a newcomer who wants to enter into the 'Horse as Healer/ Teacher' profession. She responded to an online dialogue that posed three questions:

1. Why do people keep creating new acronyms rather than using the four established ones: EGE, EFP, EAP and EAL?
2. Do you think this acronym deluge is causing problems in how you market yourself?
3. What are your thoughts on how to address this issue?"

She writes:

> "I would like to start my own program using horses to teach leadership and team building. I did a project for a marketing class, and we came up with our own acronym. EELP. Equine Executive Leadership Program. This is a totally fake acronym and was only used for the purposes of my paper. So why my own acronym? I think it speaks to everyone wanting their own identity and their own branding.
>
> If I were to use EGE, EAP, etc, I guess I would feel I was infringing on copyright? Plus I'm sure there are people out there who would be very angry if I used their acronym. It also lumps me into a category. If I wanted to do psychotherapy, I would use some acronym with psychotherapy. If I wanted to do leadership, there would be a L in my acronym. Etc.
>
> Basically it comes down to branding. (loving my marketing class lessons right now!) If an individual can create a singular and superior brand, then they can stand-alone as #1 or the best. But if they are one of many using the same acronym, the ability to be "the one and only" gets fuzzy. Comes down to competition for market share. I personally don't have these feelings, but I'm guessing some people out there do. These are just my impressions. I really have no experience with this other than theory and philosophy discussed in my MBA classes."

Her inquiry as a new professional coming into this field describes the confusion around choosing an acronym for the work she wants to do. Acronyms like Epona and EEC label the style of 'Horse as Healer/ Teacher' service one offers. They can also imply a particular lineage of educational background. Some acronyms such as EGE, EAP, and HAE describe one's professional identity, their association, and their lineage of educational background. While still others describe a service or program such as her EELP mentioned above. Without a trade name for the industry, the issue of how to properly utilize acronyms to describe professional identity, service, lineage, or association becomes overwhelming.

LACK OF A TRADE NAME FOR THE INDUSTRY AS A WHOLE

The MBA student's comments above illustrate the confusion that comes with the lack of a trade name for the 'Horse as Healer/Teacher' profession as a whole. The lack of a trade name inhibits our overall recognition for the work that we do and love. We do not have an official title that depicts the profession as a field or industry. Perhaps it is too late to create one. Perhaps we don't need one. However, as it stands now, we have forty-four descriptions for the 'Horse as Healer/Teacher' profession. I wonder how the industry will develop without a trade name to define the 'Horse as Healer/Teacher' profession. While many industry leaders, including myself, are currently discussing this issue with no resolution in sight, there are a few things you can consider in deciding on 'what to call what you do'.

Consider the coaching industry. Coaches have a trade name and a recognizable professional identity that comes with that trade name. A coach is a coach. The coach specializes in life coaching, business coaching, executive coaching, leadership coaching, etc. The coach then brands her offer with titles like Executives Leading Change, Somatics and Mastery, etc. When discussing her credentials, she refers to the particular coach school she received her certification in which offers further clarity on her stylistic approach. Within a decade the industry of coaches became widely recognized even with all of its variations and professional backgrounds.

The primary difference between the 'Horse as Healer/Teacher' profession and the coaching profession (in terms of nomenclature) is that the coaching profession has one specific brand name for the entire industry of coaches (the profession itself) that clearly delineates the type of service offered. The individual or stylistic variability of coaches is denoted by descriptive words such as life coach, business coach, executive coach, etc.

Our profession, in addition to lacking of trade name, creates further complexity by switching 'equine' for 'horse' (two words for the same animal), and adding adjectives such as assisted, facilitated, guided, or experiential (each describing our interpretation of the 'role' that the horse plays in the process). Out of the forty-four acronyms currently in use, they all have either assisted, facilitated, guided, or experiential (providing the

Ariana Strozzi

least descriptive) to describe the role of the horse (which can also be seen as the style of the work or how the horse is actually incorporated into a person's professional offer).

Maybe the 'Horse as Healer/Teacher' profession is not a profession in and of itself. Maybe it is just an additional offer one makes to their professions of psychotherapy, coaching, education, etc. If this is the case, then a professional in this field would continue to define their professional identity as a psychotherapist or coach and the acronyms they use would describe either their educational lineage and association membership or both.

THE ISSUE OF BRANDING

The topic of branding relates to how a company creates quick, sustainable recognition for its products and services. Coca Cola is a brand. Ariat is a brand. When you think of Ariat, you think of good quality leather boots and shoes meant to wear outdoors. Brand names tend to succeed when the products they represent demonstrate consistent quality and are easily recognized in the eye of the consumer.

Some acronyms listed in Appendix D are attempting to brand the professional identity and the Horse as Healer/Teacher' process (EGE), while others are branding the description of the experience (equine experiential learning). The issue of branding is further complicated by the fact that we do not have a brand name for the 'Horse as Healer/Teacher' profession. Without a unified professional title, individuals are attempting to individuate themselves from their competitors by coming up with new acronyms.

The consequence of this is forty-four acronyms and growing. Too many brand names for this industry ultimately creates confusion in the public eye. The consumer becomes distracted trying to figure out what differentiates one from the other. The common question becomes "what are the similarities and differences" between these acronyms, which ultimately takes the consumer away from focusing on the product itself; the gift of horses in teaching and healing.

The young woman in the discussion is a good example of creating further brand dilution. Will creating a new brand name for her professional identity benefit or deter her possibility for success? On one hand, her success will ultimately be determined by her ability to create and fulfill successful programs. Her success will come from her competence and producing positive results for her customers, not on what she calls herself. On the other hand, as the 'Horse as Healer/Teacher' profession develops she may experience feeling isolated from the industry as it continues to develop and unify. Her program may develop brand identity, but her professional identity may not.

In her attempt to create a brand identity, she is actually branding her program. Branding her program can be an effective way of differentiating herself <u>within</u> the 'Horse as Healer/Teacher' profession and describing her emphasis of work with executive leaders. However, it does not actually reveal her professional identity. If she becomes a certified EGE professional, she denotes her background education and alliance with a respected association in the industry. This gives her instant recognition in the industry itself and yet, she does not lose her individuality because her program still has its own brand name and description. She is able to develop her brand and her professional identity without isolating herself.

If she has no intention of attending the EGE certification program and plans to call herself an EGE professional, then her fear of being out of integrity may be grounded. Other professionals might be confused about why she is calling herself by those terms if she has not actually studied them. She has not yet addressed how she is going to be trained in this work. Having an MBA and a lifetime with horses does not qualify a person in the 'Horse as Healer/Teacher' profession. Without the vital component of a training program specifically designed to teach her how to incorporate horses into her work, she runs the risk of being incompetent in her new professional offer.

IDENTIFYING YOUR EDUCATIONAL BACKGROUND

A major topic of discussion among industry leaders is how the public and other professionals will know that incoming professionals are qualified to do this work. The more acronyms there are that are not directly identified with an association, the more concerning this issue becomes. For those of you coming into the field it will become increasingly important for you to be able to show how and with whom you learned this work.

Let's consider handicapped riding programs. They are well established in the public eye and therefore the general public would not send their child to a program that is not certified in handicapped riding. While this is not the case yet in the 'Horse as Healer/Teacher' profession, it will be within the next decade. This is part of the reason that professionals in this field want to align with either a well-established training program or association to increase customer confidence.

Many of the first generation and pioneers in this field, like myself, had no training programs available to them. They had to experiment and develop their experience and knowledge as they developed their programs and offers. Nowadays, this 'lone wolf' approach is no longer necessary, nor is it recommended. Why spend the years that it took to experiment on your own, when you can learn from the successful pioneers? If there had been a training program available when I got started, like there is now, I would have chosen a program that resonated with my philosophical perspective, my professional goals and was an active part of the growing industry.

WHAT TO CALL WHAT YOU DO

For those of you who are coming into the field, think carefully about what you are going to call your work. Make sure you differentiate your thought process in regards to how you plan to develop your professional identity (who you are and what you do) from what you might call one of your programs. Also consider, not only what you want your customers to know about you, but also what you want your peers and colleagues to know about you. Future peers and colleagues can have a positive or negative impact on your ability to succeed. By aligning with one of the well-known acronyms, other professionals will be able to have a quicker and more defined sense of your background and style of incorporating horses into your professional offer.

The public and your peers ultimately want to know with whom you studied with or how you received your knowledge and experience. When you can state recognized names and affiliations, your professional identity can blossom faster because you are leveraging their identities, rather than spending the years that it takes to create your own brand that will only dilute the industry further. Gone are the pioneering days in terms of what to call this profession. By this I do not mean that we will not enjoy many more years of growth and development in the quality and consistency of this work. There is plenty of room for continued creative expression.

I recognize the three acronyms, EGE (Equine Guided Education), EAP (Equine Assisted Psychotherapy) and EFP (Equine Facilitate Psychotherapy) over other acronyms for a number of reasons. They have been out there the longest. They each have a clear definition of meaning and interpretation. They each have roots to a well-established association. They can be sourced back to a point of origin. They have market recognition with other professionals, insurance companies and other institutions. The acronym itself stays the same when one describes 'what you do' and 'who you are'. For example, an Equine Guided Educator (EGE) does Equine Guided Education (EGE); the acronym stays the same in labeling what you do and what you offer. An Equine Assisted Psychotherapist (EAP) does Equine Assisted Psychotherapy.

When thinking of what to call yourself, first decide if you are a mental health professional, horse specialist, coach, or educator. This will help to narrow down your acronym choices. Next, study the long-standing acronyms and their affiliation with associations to choose which acronym and/or methodology best suits what you plan to offer. Reflect on what you want your professional identity to be (EGE, EFP, EAP, etc.) and which association resonates with your philosophy and approach. Hopefully, the two will relate together.

Let's look at an example of a psychotherapist with an MFCC license. She wants to do one on one work with her clients and incorporate horses into her sessions. She has decided that the EGE certification program fits her philosophy and offers the kind of training she is looking for. Once she completes the program, she lists herself as an MFCC, describing her professional expertise recognized by both her peers and the public. She further defines herself as a Certified EGE which offers more information on her training and experience in the 'Horse as Healer/Teacher' profession and her association with EGEA.

I will use myself as another example. I am a Certified Master Somatic Coach. Not everyone knows what that means. However, I do know that in the coaching industry, other professionals know that I have training in Somatics in addition to Coaching. I also have extensive experience, education and competency in leadership and life coaching. Hmm, lots of choices. I choose to describe myself as an Equine Guided Educator with credentials in Somatics and Leadership Coaching. I could choose to list myself as a Coach first and an EGE second. However, I am choosing, very purposefully to list myself as an EGE first and a Coach secondarily (via further credentials that describe my coach and somatic expertise). To further define my offer, I have my branded Leadership & Horses™ program.

Next I discuss the three well-known associations that directly relate to the 'Horse as Healer/Teacher' professions. Each of the associations listed have been in business for over five years since the beginning of 2009. Please note that I asked each association to provide the following information to best represent their organization as of the beginning of 2009. They have approved the following descriptions.

EGE AND EGEA

EGE stands for Equine Guided Education, coined by Ariana Strozzi in 1999, and is supported and acknowledged by the Equine Guided Education Association, which was officially formed in 2003 after several years of research and development. EGE incorporates the sensate, intuitive wisdom of horses into human growth, learning and development. It is available to people (from all walks of life) and can be facilitated by a mental health professional, a coach, or other type of educator.

EGEA offers membership, educational programs, certification, continuing education, an annual conference, an Internet library, an associate network, a Code of Ethics, and support for professionals and the public. In fact, EFMHA liked EGEA's standards and Code of Ethics so much, they asked to include some of the material in their Code of Ethics.

EGEA's vision is to re-connect people to land and nature through various 'Horse as Healer/Teacher' learning models so that each can support the other. The mission of the Equine Guided Education Association (EGEA) is to create and support a unified discourse involving the interaction of the horse as a respected 'guide' in human growth, learning and development. Members include coaches, educators, consultants, mental health professionals, holistic health educators, human development facilitators, teachers, alternative education specialists, horse trainers, riding instructors, human resources professionals, etc. EGEA offers a certification program for incoming and established professionals. Please visit www.equineguidededucation.org for more details.

EAP AND EAGALA

The Equine Assisted Growth and Learning Association was founded in 1999 to provide education, standards, innovation, and support to professionals providing services in Equine Assisted Psychotherapy (EAP) and Equine Assisted Learning (EAL). The organization provides hands-on training program and certification, conducts annual conferences in the U.S. and Europe, publishes a magazine, and provides other educational and promotional resources for EAP/EAL.

EAGALA states that, "Equine Assisted Learning (EAL) is an acronym associated with EAGALA. Although EAL has remained a part of EAGALA from it's beginning, EAP is more often identified with EAGALA. Additionally, EAGALA's standard of a licensed mental health professional involved in all sessions applies to EAL as well. According to EAGALA, the purpose for this is to provide an additional safeguard respecting the power of this work even when there is not a psychotherapy focus and the need to understand boundaries and other ethical concerns that are part of a licensed clinician's training."

EAGALA standards include a focus on ground exercises (not riding), solution-oriented approach, a team comprised of a mental health professional, equine specialist, and horse(s) (in the arena with clients at all times), and a Code of Ethics. EAGALA also has an Ethics Committee and protocol in place to address any concerns that are reported about certified members, which assists in setting a standard and reputation of quality and excellence. EAGALA offers a certification program. To learn more visit www.eagala.org.

EFP AND EFMHA

EFMHA is a section of NARHA (formerly known as the North American Riding for the Handicapped Association). Equine Facilitated Psychotherapy (EFP) is experiential psychotherapy that includes equines.

EFP is facilitated by a licensed, credentialed mental health professional working with an appropriately credentialed equine professional. EFP incorporates established treatment goals and objectives developed by the therapist in conjunction with the client. The therapist must be an appropriately credentialed mental health professional to legally practice psychotherapy and EFP. EFMHA does not have any official training or certification programs, however they are working on a pilot program for equine specialists. They are currently in the process of re-defining their vision, mission and objectives, so visit their website for details, www.narha.org.

EAHAE

The European Association for Horse Assisted Education was formed in 2004 by Gerhard and Karin Krebs to provide a membership association for professionals in Europe to collaborate and develop HAE. Horse Assisted Education (HAE) incorporates horses into self-development and leadership models. EAHAE offers an Internet platform and an annual conference. The organization is run as a HorseDream™ non-profit center. To learn more visit www.eahae.org.

SUMMARY

It would seem natural to assume that acronyms that use the term, 'assisted', imply an alignment to EAGALA philosophies; acronyms with the term, 'facilitate', imply alignment with EFMHA philosophies; and acronyms with the term, 'guided' imply alignment with EGEA philosophies. This does not mean that the respective organizations approve of the acronyms being used, nor the professionals using those terms. Regardless of one's opinion on the matter, if you use one of these three terms in your acronyms, other professionals will tend to associate you with the corresponding association.

Unusual acronyms to describe your professional title may not stand the test of time as the industry works to collaborate on universal language and terminology. This issue of acronym deluge is currently a topic of discussion among the three associations (EAGALA, EGEA, and EFMHA). Over the next five to ten years, it is anticipated that there will be more structure and standardization of this industry. My advice to anyone coming into the field is to align themselves with one or more of the current associations and avoid 'lone-wolfing' it. This will allow you to keep abreast of the evolution and changes occurring in the field as well as being able to contribute to its development.

SPECIAL NOTE

Both EFMHA and EGEA agree that it is important to refrain from the terms 'using' the horse, or the horse is a 'tool'. The horse is not a tool, or prop. The horse is a sentient being with feelings, thoughts, emotions, memories and empathetic abilities. Other ways to describe the work is to use terms like, 'interacting' with horses, or 'working' with horses. I tell my students to be very careful about these terms, as I have seen many occasions when a newcomer to the field is energetically dismissed or judged because they used either the term 'use' or 'tool' in reference to horses.

MY STORY BEHIND EGEA

(Excerpted from an article written for EFMHA magazine titled, "Finding a Place to Belong", 2004, by Ariana Strozzi)

It's amazing to me how fast the application of the horse's innate wisdom and heart has expanded into the domains of human growth and learning. For so many years, I felt alone teaching concepts of authenticity, trust, intention, and intuition through the eyes of the horse. My students would ask me if I knew of other people doing this work. "I imagine there may be some people out there, but I don't know who and where they are." I would say. It wasn't until late 1999 that people began to send me newspaper clippings or other written material about folks applying horse logic to prisoners, to medical students, and to youth at risk.

One day, a student of mine came to the ranch for her monthly EGE session. She was a psychologist and had been interning and studying to become qualified in EGE. As she was catching me up with her recent adventures, she announced, "I am now a certified equine therapist." There was a question mark behind her tone, as if she herself wondered what that meant. I had never heard of an Equine Therapist, so I asked her, "Does that mean that you are a therapist to the horse?"

"No, no", she replied, "It's similar to the work you do with humans and horses. In Equine Therapy there is a horse specialist and a therapist during the session." Many months later, she asked me to do a clinic in her area. She had enrolled several people who claimed to be equine therapists. What I witnessed were that most of these folks had very little horse experience and no official training to be working with people on an emotional or spiritual level. For the first time, I felt fear about this body of work that I am so deeply passionate about and committed to.

My feelings were mixed. I felt both a sense of, 'finally the world sees the profound role horses play as teachers and healers to humans'. On the other hand, I worried, 'What if these new people don't know what they are doing and someone gets hurt emotionally or physically? What if the public walks away from a program or facilitator thinking it was too weird and this new discourse disappears before it had a chance?' At the end of the day I ended our session as a spokeswoman of the vision of what is possible for humans and horses and advised these people to find a teacher/mentor who confirms that they are ready to do this work.

These innocent newcomers to the complex field of equine emotional, spiritual, biological and psychological awareness had no idea how silly it sounded to me that someone could be certified in just three days. Will they be able to identify and deal with the dramatic shift in a horse's state of being in the presence of emotional incongruence or inauthentic expression? Will they know what to do when a horse mirrors unresolved trauma in a person's body? Having witnessed several thousand human/horse interactions since 1990, and continually awed by the depth of insight and sixth sense that horses bring to humans, I couldn't help but think, 'they have no idea what they are getting into.' Will they be able to protect the horse and the human when there is emotional, physical or psychological incongruence present? Do they even know what that means?

As I left the dusty arena in California that day, I began a quest to find the answer to these questions. As I researched EAGALA and

EFMHA, I tried to understand the difference between Equine Facilitated Psychotherapy and Equine Assisted Psychotherapy. I figured that if I was confused about the difference, then surely the public was as well. I enrolled in various training programs in order to experience the work myself so that I could have an informed opinion about each type.

I joined EAGALA and EFMHA, but didn't really feel like I belonged. I didn't seem to fit in the category of EFP or EAP because I am not a licensed psychotherapist. I am a Certified Master Somatic Coach, I have a degree in Zoology, and at the time I had 39 years of experience working with horses, 18 years working with human education through experiential practices with horses, and 13 years as a 4H Horse Leader. Even though I was on the certification team for EFMHA, they told me I would never be able to be certified by the very standards I help set, because I am not a licensed psychotherapist.

To further complicate my search for a herd–a place to connect– prospective students continued to ask me where they could belong if they were not psychotherapists. They consistently felt like EAGALA and EFMHA were not the right fit for them because they did not consider themselves to be mental health professionals, and they were not just equine specialists. They would often say, "Why don't YOU start an association?" And so, nudged by the blossoming field of "Horse as Healer/Teacher", I felt pressed to explore a bigger container for the diversity of this work.

I imagined a blank canvas and I imagined what the painting of 'Horse as Healer/Teacher' would look like fifty years from now. I asked myself the question, "What if we could start from the beginning and find a name that would cover all of the different styles of this work?"

I imagined a unified field where we would have a unified name and be able to say, "I am an Equine Guided Educator (EGE)." Like all chiropractors simply state, "I am a chiropractor." As I thought about the adjectives used to describe the work such as facilitated, experiential, assisted, my heart kept saying, "Horses do more than facilitate and they are more than assistants. They literally 'guide' the process." If the horse says, "pay attention here," I can't imagine a situation in which we, as facilitators, would choose not to follow the horse's lead.

Ariana Strozzi

When we allow horses to 'guide' us into a psycho spiritual landscape, we are providing more than an equine experience. If and when we are ready, the horse even guides us into a mythical landscape far beyond words, another realm of consciousness that is ancient and indigenous to the land.

Persistently pursued by the next generation of educators to define and create standards for this work, I assembled several independent groups of equine/human educators to discuss a broader brushstroke to equine/human education. We researched the best adjective to describe the respectful application of 'Horse as Healer/Teacher' to human growth and learning. We researched the definitions of the following the words:

Guide: Implies intimate knowledge of the course or way and all of its difficulties and dangers. Synonyms include: direct, escort, lead, pilot, shepherd, show, steer; to set upon one's way. The noun 'guide' means -someone who takes one through unknown or unexplored territory.

Experiential: A personal reality; existential: derived from experience or the experience of existence.

Facilitate: To make easy or less difficult.

Assist: To give support, help or aid.

Educate: To develop or cultivate in mind and character. Synonyms include: to train, develop, prepare, school, cultivate.

Education: Discipline of mind or character through study or instruction; dealing with the principles and practices of teaching and learning.

The term Education seemed better than learning because it not only includes a wide variety of learning models including therapy and coaching, but it also includes the element of teaching. Its definition includes the principles and practices of developing 'the self'. The word,

Guide, offers the best possible definition of what the horse actually does, whether we are doing therapy, coaching, or basic horsemanship. It also feels most respectful to the horse and gives the horse the more predominant role in the work. We, humans, merely translate (well or poorly) what the horse is mirroring in an EGE session. The horse is the crucial element; the one who reflects the essential elements of spirit and inner-psyche dilemmas.

So after many years of exploration I felt like I belonged. I am an Equine Guided Educator and I do Equine Guided Education. The acronym EGE works for both descriptions of who I am and what I do. And so, EGEA was formed. We have received tremendous support from EAGALA and EFMHA over the years.

Ariana Strozzi

HUMAN AND HORSE SKILLS REQUIRED

The following descriptions are recommended skill sets for anyone doing 'Horse as Healer/Teacher' work. They do not necessarily cover specific skills for psychotherapists or coaches. This chapter is meant to help offer clarification on the kind of skills one needs to have competency in before becoming a professional EGE. As I mentioned earlier, I will be using the term EGE for convenience and if you go by another acronym the following chapter may still be useful in evaluating your qualifications. More discussion of skill sets is mentioned in the following chapter on "Choosing a Training Program."

FACILITATION SKILLS

- Demonstrated experience in coaching, educational or psychotherapy methods
- Knowledge of adventure-based experiences
- Understand the impact of the setting, atmosphere and staff attitudes on client
- Knowledge of set up, process and debriefing of equine experiences
- Knowledge of the boundaries between coaching and therapy
- Adapts to immediate circumstances and needs of client within the framework established
- Maintains standards of confidentiality
- Demonstrated experience in Horse/Human interactions
- Understands risk factors and safety protocols of equine activities
- Understands human projection onto equines

Relates metaphors and horse reflections to client's goals and concerns

 Evaluates effectiveness of sessions in terms of meeting client goals

 Evaluates facility, staff, and equines in terms of appropriateness for specific client

 Practices within area of expertise

 Competent to manage staff to ensure consistent handling of horses and process

EQUINE INTERACTION SKILLS

 Knowledge of:

- ❈ Equine behavior
- ❈ Social hierarchal, herd nature and instinct
- ❈ What the horse is responding to and why
- ❈ Herd behavior
- ❈ Horse related equipment, tools and techniques
- ❈ Horse physiology and anatomy
- ❈ Horse terminology regarding tack, breeds, recreational disciplines, etc.
- ❈ Horse management and care including stabling and feeding options
- ❈ Different equine training methods and philosophies
- ❈ Safety issues when around horses and inherent risks involved with horses

- Can interpret horse behavior effectively—Equine Experience over several years and with numerous horses. (See section on how much horse experience do I need to have in the next chapter)

- Understands, listens to and trusts body language, senses and instincts of horses

- Manages the physical, emotional and instinctive needs of horses

- Competent to provide consistent, non-violent horsemanship handling techniques to clients/students that are in the presence of horses

- Able to manage feeding, watering, exercise regimes, pasture and housing requirements for horses

- Understands Equine/Human experience and dynamics

- Understands and competent to deal with horses that respond to incongruences of humans that can be intensified by abuse histories, unresolved trauma and pathology

- Identifies and addresses immediately any anxiety, stress or threat or gestures of horses

- Qualified in at least five specific horse/human activities including moving horses as a group/herd, walking in hand, lunging, grooming, driving, bathing, trail course, etc.

- Recognizes and manages mental health of horse

- Competent to handle and calm spooky, nervous or aggressive horses

- Can easily maneuver in a herd of horses

You may also refer to the Code of Ethics for EGEA in appendix C for more details.

HOW MUCH HORSE EXPERIENCE DO YOU NEED TO HAVE?

Because of the inherent risks involved with equine activities it is essential that an experienced equine specialist be present at any process in which a student/client is near or around horses. If you are not a horse expert, then you need to partner with someone who is. Even with an equine specialist present, you need to have some experience with horses. You need to be comfortable around horses and understand the basic safety issues associated with them. Any equine specialist you decide to work with also needs to have experienced Equine Guided Education as a participant, or better yet be certified in EGE as well.

How do you know if you have enough horse experience? If you choose a competent teacher in EGE, they should be able to assess your level of experience and offer additional resources for gaining horse competency. If you want to consider yourself as a horse specialist, consider that you need a minimum of 5000 hours with horses (this is equivalent to 10 hours per week for 10 years) and have worked with at least 50 different horses. If you do not have that level of experience, then you should consider working with someone who does while you are developing your equine competency.

WHAT ARE THE ETHICAL REASONS TO BECOME CERTIFIED?

The unique and profound opportunities of bringing horses to people for the sake of growth and learning is both exciting and serious. Horses can become unpredictable and aggressive around incongruent emotions and energies within their environment. While a person may be competent with horses and/or human development, incorporating the two requires a whole new set of competencies. It is important to respect the horses and humans as sensate beings, each with their own unique perspective. The safety of the horse and human—emotionally, physically and spiritually—is an important and sensitive matter. One can never have too much competency in this area. Therefore, there is no good reason not to get certified.

It is important to respect what experts in the field who are committed to developing this discourse have already learned. The public as well as other professionals will increasingly expect you to have qualified training in your area of expertise.

Ariana Strozzi

While some professionals may have extensive horsemanship and coaching skills, the EGE process creates a whole new paradigm for learning. The EGE process is complex and transcends traditional learning models. A complete paradigm shift in consciousness is required. Emotional, psychological and spiritual concerns may arise at any given moment. Allowing the horse to be the 'guide' on the learning path is more sensitive, intimate and personal than traditional forms of coaching/ therapy.

An EGE professional needs to be skilled in recognizing even the slightest shifts in states of mind and energetic responses in the horse, human and environment at any given moment. It is essential to have experience or knowledge in the EGE process before attempting to facilitate the process. Even for professionals with extensive horsemanship skills, one must unlearn many of the horsemanship skills they have been taught in order for EGE to be successful. For a person to be in integrity with this work they need to be educated in it. This is so for equine specialists, coaches and therapists.

In the 1990's specific opportunities to educate oneself in this field did not exist. But now there are several good programs out there offering training and certification. There is no good reason to spend the years that it takes to learn the nuances of this work on your own when you can learn from a certification program. In addition, within the next few years, the public will become increasingly savvy about asking for your qualifications and certification. Think about the handicapped riding industry—the public does not consider going to a person offering handicapped riding services if they are not certified. It is common knowledge today to expect a handicapped riding professional to be certified. This is how it will be in this industry over the next few years.

CHOOSING A TRAINING PROGRAM

As I mentioned in the chapter on "What to Call What You Do?" there are basically three predominant 'Horse as Healer/Teacher' models that you can choose from to get started. I will discuss some of the more well-established certification programs that are recognized by the more seasoned professionals in the field. Other programs exist, but I had a hard time finding a consistent referral or description for them to include in this chapter. Remember that this field is tremendously variable. My goal in this chapter is to offer you a way to think, plan and prepare your education in 'Horse as Healer/Teacher' education.

For simplicity sake, I am going to focus on training programs that teach you how to incorporate horses into learning models distinct from how to get yourself educated in horsemanship and/or human development. As far as training to gain competency with horses and with people there is tremendous variability again and it is too complex a matter to discuss here. I am going to assume in this chapter that you have already gained the appropriate credentials in working with people, whether your focus is therapy, coaching or general education.

If you do not already have extensive equine or human development skill you should not expect to become competent to work with people and horses by taking a couple of workshops or even in a certification program alone. You will need additional training and experience in either horsemanship or human development or both. You can still take EGE training programs for your own self-development, to experience EGE, and to help you determine if this is the kind of work you really want to get into.

By becoming a certified Equine Guided Educator you demonstrate through curriculum vitae and completion in an Equine Guided Education program that you have completed a course of study directly related to incorporating horses into a specific method of learning. For example, if you are an equine specialist who completes a certification program you can become an Equine Guided Educator who is competent as an equine specialist. This does not qualify you to provide coaching or therapy to the public. You may provide horsemanship education with a beginning knowledge of the broader ramifications of self-development though the 'eyes of the horse'.

If you are a certified coach or licensed psychotherapist and you do not have extensive equine experience, upon completion of a certification program you can become an Equine Guided Educator who works within your competency as a coach or therapist. It will be important to work with a qualified equine specialist until you are competent with horses. Review some of the skill sets of an Equine Guided Educator from both facilitative and equine points of view later in this chapter and the section on the Code of Ethics for EGEA to help you discern more details.

A WORD OF ADVICE

Avoid "Train the Trainer" programs that are popping up across the country in which the facilitators have only been doing this work for less than five years. Three to five day "Train the Trainer" programs generally imply that you are already a trainer or professional. These programs might be a good way to continue your learning once you have completed a rigorous course of study or have your certification, but they will not provide you with adequate training on their own. You will be exposed to new things and new ideas (sounds fun), but you will not get the in-depth, recurrent study and practice of specific skill sets in horsemanship and facilitation that you need to be great at this work.

Avoid programs in which the training programs listed on the website have no actual dates. This usually means the person does not have a lot of potential students and are hoping that they'll get enough interest to put together a program. This is not the sign of a seasoned, experienced teacher.

I don't think a person is qualified to teach other people how to do this work until they have been doing it as a full-time professional (as their main source of income) for at least eight years. It takes extensive experience to truly understand the complexity of the work itself and the potentially unexpected and dangerous outcomes that can arise. I think it is absolutely imperative that a person coming into this field has a deep-seated, humble respect for the vast range of potential outcomes of this work. Over 95% of the time, the process seems to run smoothly and the work is both profound and magical. However, there are occasions that arise (quite unexpectedly) in which the horse becomes unusually aggressive. I've heard numerous stories of the 'gentlest horse known to man' becoming dangerous in a split second (something the horse handler never thought could ever happen).

Developing the wisdom to 'expect the unexpected' and make practical decisions on appropriate facilitation takes experience. Until, someone has encountered the vast range of expressions this work can take, they should not be teaching others how to do it because they have not experienced it in its entirety.

Remember, it is one set of skills to be qualified to provide opportunities for learning to the public. It is another competency entirely to 'teach' someone HOW to DO IT. So choose your teacher (and thus the program) based on the style of facilitation they EMBODY and the competency they have to TEACH the skills you want to learn. Later in this chapter I will discuss further some the criteria to consider before choosing a program or teacher to learn this work from.

There is no governing body that determines who is qualified to do this work, teach this work or what programs are legitimate. At this time there are three organizations that are working hard to develop their interpretation of this work and each one is stylistically different. EAGALA and EFMHA tend toward psychotherapy and process style facilitation, while EGEA tends toward coaching style facilitation. In the chapter on "What to Call What You Do?", I discuss these organizations in more detail.

Every dollar you spend on your education will provide you with important knowledge. This is not an arena to pinch pennies on. Usually the really good programs are going to be more expensive, because the professionals offering them are serious about their work, they have invested a tremendous amount of time and money on their own education, and they are experienced, seasoned teachers who know the value of their programs and have proven success. Spend good money, invest in yourself on a program that will actually train you in the work, not just provide a few tidbits of information.

I know that some people have a hard time with the financial commitment and the trial of leaving ranch and pets to go off and study. But, think of it as an investment in yourself. I bet that if you sit down with pad and paper, and project how many new customers you can work with once you are certified that your financial investment will be returned in increased sales and income within the first three to six months of your certification. And think of the value of 'getting away' from your day-to-day commitments to study yourself and develop your future business. How often do you take that kind of time? I try to go on a learning adventure several times a year. I find it to be tremendously inspiring, and helps me re-connect to my life purpose and passion.

FINDING A CERTIFICATION PROGRAM THAT MEETS YOUR NEEDS

Before going out and actually choosing a program, do some self-inquiry. Explore the following questions:

SELF-INQUIRY:

1. What are my goals for this work?
   a. What types of people do I want to work with?
   b. What are some of their common issues or obstacles to change?
   c. Will I be working primarily with individuals or in group settings?
2. What style of facilitation suits me best? A therapy model or a coaching model? If you are not sure go out and experience one of each. Also see notes in appendix.
3. What are some specific topics that I have already identified that I want to learn more about? (This could be business development, types of exercises, etc).

You do not have to know the answers to all of these questions to choose a program or to be accepted in it per se, but if you do have some clarity on these questions, you will have a better sense of what to ask when you are interviewing a potential program and/or teacher.

INTERVIEW THE PROGRAM TEACHER/FACILITATOR:

Here are some questions that you can ask.

1. My background is (...fill in...) and my goals are (.... fill in...). Will your program help me to achieve this and how?
2. What does the 'Horse as Healer/Teacher' process entail from your perspective?
3. What role or part does the horse play in the process?
4. What would you say is your style of facilitation?
5. What area of human growth and development do you specialize in?
6. How many years have you been doing this work?
7. Is this work how you make your living or are you doing other work as well?
8. How many years have you been teaching this work to other professionals?
9. Where did you get your training and/or certification?
10. Do you have any previous students/clients that I could speak to about the program?

PERSONAL NOTES:

1. Do you have a good feeling when you speak with this person?
2. Do you feel like you resonate with their philosophy?

EGEA CERTIFICATION PROGRAM

Excerpted from the EGEA Website 2009

The founder of Equine Guided Education, Ariana Strozzi, has been incorporating horses into self-development and leadership programs since 1990. Ariana Strozzi and EGEA faculty have been teaching professionals how to incorporate horses into their professional offers since 1998. Professionals who enroll in the certification program include coaches, therapists, educators, horse trainers, equestrians, teachers, college students, animal communicators, and individuals who are focused on their own self-development.

The certification program is for new as well as seasoned professionals. For new people coming into this field, you do not have to know exactly how you plan to incorporate horses into your work in order to enter our certification program. You will gain that clarity during the program and upon completion have a concrete sense of how you want to incorporate horses into your offer. For seasoned professionals, you can avoid the four to six year learning curve it will take for you to figure this work out on your own as well as continuing your own professional development.

Participants of the certification program come from a wide variety of backgrounds and experience. Our goal is to encourage you to refine your existing skills as well as learn new skills. We are not focused on one particular methodology, but rather on the universal application of what horses can offer to healing and teaching models. The program is open to professionals from other disciplines including EAP, EAL and EFL.

We pride ourselves on the success of our students. Our intent is not on how many students we enroll in our programs, but rather that the students in our programs gain the skills they need and come out of our program with confidence and clarity. Because this is a learning-by-doing program, you will not only learn how to incorporate horses into your offer, you will come away with clear goals and objectives for your personal and professional life.

Bringing horses into the learning model, creates a whole new set of complexities and unknowns. We teach you how to think, how to trust yourself and your horses, and how to navigate in a wide variety of situations. The program includes the somatic (non-verbal) perspective of horses that make this work possible. We focus on developing your ability to observe, recognize, and articulate these dynamics.

Our program is tried and true. Professionals who graduate from our certification program go on to run successful programs of their own around the world. We encourage our students to stay in touch with us and offer continuing mentoring whenever they need it. In addition, graduates of the EGE certification program can become Associate Members of the EGEA.

Ariana Strozzi

EAGALA CERTIFICATION PROGRAM

Excerpted from the EAGALA website

The EAGALA Certification process involves a learning structure with two certification levels, EAGALA Certification and EAGALA Advanced Certification.

EAGALA CERTIFICATION

You must complete Fundamentals of EAGALA Model Practice Training Part 1 (3 day course); submit a Professional Development Portfolio, Complete Fundamentals of EAGALA Model Practice Training Part 2 (3 day course).

EAGALA ADVANCED CERTIFICATION

You must complete EAGALA Certification as described above, complete Fundamentals of EAGALA Model Practice Training Part 1 a second time as a returnee, attend one EAGALA Annual Conference, submit an article that is accepted for publication in EAGALA News, complete 150 hours of EAGALA client sessions (post EAGALA Certification) with Mentoring, Complete Advanced Training requirement (determined through Mentoring).

For more information please visit: http://www.eagala.org.

OTHER PROGRAMS

There are other programs out there besides EGEA and EAGALA offering education and/or certification in the 'Horse as Healer/Teacher' professions. I will mention a few of them briefly in this section. Again, the purpose of this book is to help you think about your options. In this chapter, I am taking a 'birds eye' view; a quick glance. There are some great teachers out there offering certification in their particular method of 'Horse as Healer/Teacher' work. The reason why I included a bit more detail of EGEA and EAGALA is to give you an idea of the type of material you will be reviewing when you research your options. Hopefully, it will help you clarify your questions before you begin your interviews. Also, these two associations have a very clearly delineated course of study and have been offering their certification programs for an extended period of time.

Barbara Rector offers her Adventures in Awareness™ program. Barbara is a gifted pioneer in this field and is a co-founder of EFMHA. To learn more about her programs visit, www.adventuresinawareness.net. Linda Kohanov, famous author of the *"Tao of Equus"* and *"Riding Between the Worlds"* offers Epona Approved Instructor Training programs. To learn more visit her site at www.taoofequus.com. Gerhard and Karin Krebs, in Germany and founder of EAHAE offer a HorseDream program, to visit them go to www.eahae.org.

SUCCESSFUL SKILL SETS OF
A BUSINESS OWNER

Establishing and managing a business requires focus, mental toughness, resilience, tenacity, self-direction, commitment, trust, intuition, intention, independence, creativity, curiosity and faith. If you are becoming self-employed for the first time, you might want to consider hiring a coach to help you make the transition into being your own boss. The daily, monthly and yearly activities required of a small business owner are dramatically different than those who are employed.

As the owner, boss, employee, and visionary you need to be prepared to perform all of the roles of a small company including administration (answering phones, database management, filing papers) managing marketing schedules and materials, finances, sales, fulfilling on the offers of the business, forecasting, etc. Even if you have plenty of money to hire people for these roles, you still have to create the roles and oversee them.

I don't mean to sound discouraging. Owning your own business is tremendously exciting and rewarding. You can do what you 'love' to do. You have control of how often you want to work, who you want to work with and how much money you want to make. In the following paragraphs I will offer a few comments on some of the qualities I see one needs to practice in order to be successful in business. These qualities are also the qualities of a leader–one who is directing their life on purpose. These skills can be developed and practiced. You do not have to be born with them. These skills are studied in both the Leadership & Horses™ programs and the EGE Certification Program because they are non-verbal communicators that are universal to both horses and humans.

As a business owner you make offers to others through written and verbal communication. Your offers are either accepted or declined by your potential customers. The customer's decision to accept your offer is based, not just on the words you use to describe your offer, but more importantly on how the customer 'feels' about your competency, your sincerity, your reliability and ultimately your ability to fulfill on your offer. They need to believe you are good on your word. Customers make these decisions based on how you embody the non-verbal communication cues mentioned below. Customers determine if they trust you, believe you, and if you can help them accomplish some change. Potential customers will not enroll in your programs or offers if they do not believe you or if they think you do not believe yourself.

The following nine skills are essential to making offers and having your offers accepted. Your potential customers are looking for you to embody these qualities. Please note that most of these concepts are discussed in more depth in my first book, *"Horse Sense For The Leader Within."*

CURIOSITY

Curiosity is the home of imagination and creativity. A business owner without curiosity is like a fish without water. Curiosity is a form of passion, an aliveness towards life. We start dreaming about owning our own business through our imagination. By nurturing our imagination, our business concept blossoms. We imagine who we want to work with, how we want to work with them including the themes we want to focus on. We imagine how much income we want to make, how often we want to work, etc.

Once we have established our business, our curiosity towards our customers becomes a fundamental aspect to our success. Imagining who our customers are and what they need informs decisions on how we make and package our offers. The world our customers live in changes continuously. Therefore it is reasonable to expect the needs of the market (our potential customer base) to change. Bringing our curiosity and imagination to the changing needs of your customers, will be essential to your continued success over time.

The practice of applying your imagination also helps you in determining potential risks to success, short term and long-term product/service viability, problem solving, and shaping your offer to meet the needs of your customers.

A POSITIVE MENTAL ATTITUDE

You are able to stay optimistic even when things don't happen right away or your offer is declined. It takes an average of two years for a business to start showing signs that it's going to succeed.

I like to think of a new store in your local town. You go to town frequently and one day you see a new storefront. You've walked down this street many times over the years and seen businesses come and go. You might look in the window as you walk by and think to yourself, "Oh, that store looks interesting. I wonder if it will make it."

Six months go by, you walk by the new store several times and one day you think to yourself, "Wow, it's still in business. I wonder what they have in there. I should go in there sometime." And so you walk on. Another six months go by (so now it as been a year) you walk by and say, "Oh yeah, I should really go in there one of these days." A year later you actually walk in the store. It took two years for you, the customer, to actually check out the store's offer.

Be prepared to put your business offer out there and not get an immediate response. It may take awhile for your potential customers to take your business seriously.

INTENTION

An intense desire to bring your concept forward, in spite of risks, fear of the unknown, or fear of failure will take you far. This trait is so important that if you don't have it, find it. This main ingredient will carry you through your fears and any windy turns you encounter on your path to success. It will inspire you as well as others. Think of your intention like your energy or life force propelling you into the future of your design, like fuel powers an engine.

Your intention (your passion for your offer) is contagious and is what ultimately attracts potential customers and creates an opportunity for them to learn more. They can feel your enthusiasm in the work you are offering when you discuss it with them or observe you in action. The first level of engagement with a potential customer happens when they become interested in learning more about what you do and how you do it.

INTUITION

Applying your intuition to your business decisions is an important skill that should not be taken for granted. If you listen to your intuition, it will tell you where and when to make your offer, who to make your offer to, when a customer is really not interested in your offer, or when they really are. Your intuition will also come into play when you are on the phone with potential customers, you can listen between the words and sense what they are looking for, distinct from what they say they are looking for.

Some of the most successful business owners I have ever met, when asked how they made tough decisions repeatedly replied, "I just had a gut feeling about it." Often, their gut feeling /intuition is what they followed in starting their business, especially new and unproven business offers. They followed a feeling that what they saw and what they wanted to offer was important and of value.

SELF-CONFIDENCE

Self-confidence happens when you are not worrying about how you are doing. You are not self-conscious or doubting yourself. This doesn't mean that you won't occasionally have self-judgments or doubts. It means that you do not allow your negative self-perceptions to stop you from reaching for your dreams. If you do not have confidence in your offer, your potential customers will not either. So it is very important to nurture your own belief that you have an important offer to make and that you will succeed.

Self-confidence shows up as a deep-seated belief or sureness in yourself. A lead mare in a herd gains respect because she has confidence (no doubt) in who she is and the decisions she makes. Just like the horses in her herd trust her decisions, your future customers will accept your offer when they can sense that you are sure about yourself and what you believe in.

TRUST

Trust is fundamental. Without trust conversations are rarely productive. Relationships do not develop. Contracts are not signed. Trust is developed through conversations, negotiations, requests, offers, etc. Closing the sale (the customers accepts your offer and puts their money on the table) happens when you have built enough trust with them that they believe you can accomplish what you say is possible.

Your trust in the value of your offer and your ability/competency to fulfill on your offers is vital to your success. Having trust, a deep-seated faith, that you will be successful is a practice. When you find yourself doubting your abilities, or your decision to go into business, find a way back to your faith, your internal trust meter. If you don't trust yourself, no one else will.

Your first customers will enroll in your offer based on minimal trust (which basically means that they want to trust you). Trust is initiated by the culmination of your self-confidence, passion and follow through on what you say is possible. As you produce positive and impactful results, your own trust (or faith) will develop as well as your customers' trust. Trust is further developed by producing consistent and reliable results and becomes the primary factor in creating referral business; your best and most valuable marketing tool.

FOLLOW THROUGH ON COMMITMENTS

Follow through requires mental toughness, determination and strong belief that what you are doing is important for the greater good. Your ability to follow through on your commitments will determine the success of your business. Your business will not succeed on wishful thinking, great hopes, beautiful graphics or a fancy website. The marketplace will sense, just like horses do, if you are really going to follow through on your new offer. Just like the story at the beginning of the chapter, people will often wait to see if you really mean business.

For example, when you see websites that offer public programs with no dates, it does not instill confidence that the program is really thriving. One wonders, "Why don't they have any dates listed? Are they not sure they will be successful? Do they have enough customers to actually be in business? Hmm, I'm not sure I want to participate then." Therefore, make a commitment and follow through. Success will follow. Be patient. It takes time to build that next level of trust mentioned in the previous virtue and can only be done by your follow-through and performance.

COMPETENCY

Competency to fulfill on your offer seems obvious. Customer satisfaction in your ability to provide the service you are promoting is the fundamental ingredient to business growth. Customers who are satisfied with the results of your service will tell others, providing important word of mouth referrals to future potential customers. This is ultimately how your business will grow and flourish. When you are competent at something you 'embody' the material you are presenting. People interpret your competency by your presence or 'way of being'.

SUMMARY

Ask yourself if you are ready to practice the skills set forth in this chapter. If and when you doubt yourself, revisit this chapter, re-commit to the practices and 'get back on the horse'. Like my grandfather used to say, "If you fall off of your horse, the first thing you need to do is get back on." His advice has proven to be a useful metaphor in any venture that requires commitment, perseverance and will power.

Another practice is to reflect upon someone who is a business owner whom you admire. Why do you admire them? Do they exhibit all or some of these traits? This person can be a role model for you when you need that extra incentive to stay the course. I am a firm believer in the saying, "Where there is a will there is a way!" It might not happen overnight, but if you stay the course, develop the skills you need, and believe that you can do it, you will.

PREPARING A BUSINESS PLAN

A business plan is a written document that describes your business in detail. It includes what services/products the business offers and to whom, how it plans to succeed, and defines the reason why it will be an important and worthy business. It is a written forecast of the potential economic viability of your business. It will help you define your goals and objectives and provide you with areas you may need to do further research.

If you want to study how to write a business plan in more detail, I suggest you go online (I have provided some good sources at the end of this chapter) or to a bookstore or library and pick up a couple of books on the subject. In this chapter I am going to offer a basic type of business plan.

As a business owner since 1986, I have found it to be tremendously valuable to write a business plan that I can refer back to and gauge my success at reaching my goals. Writing a business plan has helped me to gain clarity on my intentions and goals for my business and has also helped me to locate areas of importance that I need to investigate further before making strategic decisions. When I need to make a major decision about re-shaping an offer or service that my business offers, I revisit my business plan and sometimes even re-write it.

It has been very rewarding to go back and review my strategic goals and elements within my business plan and see that I have achieved my goals. It is also rewarding to have done the research needed to accomplish the business plan because I am able to refer back to it when it is time to re-assess and re-define the next direction for the business. It's like I have already done my homework. The template is already there to add to, to refine and to redirect as needed.

Once you have a business plan, an even more valuable practice is to review it at the beginning of each New Year. Each year, I don't necessarily re-write my plan, but I do review if I am on track. I make changes and project how I would like to see the business develop over the next one, three and five years. If you have already done your own business plan, then just review the following reflections and see if there are any areas of particular interest that will help you spur your thoughts and galvanize your thinking.

If you are planning a non-profit organization, a business plan must be much more rigorous and I advise you to consult with an expert in non-profits or at least research business plan requirements from a non-profit perspective. The following reflection-based questions can still offer you a more personal perspective that is YOUR personal business plan. If the thought of writing a business plan is overwhelming, I suggest hiring a coach or gathering a few friends or colleagues together to help you get started.

The very first step in preparing a business plan is to do the first and second level reflections in this chapter. First consider these reflections from a personal (I, me) point of view. Once you have completed this, review the first and second level reflections from your business's point of view. In addition to these reflection exercises, you will need to examine and reflect upon the third level reflections. I have listed two of the more personal third level reflections in this chapter. They are your curriculum vitae and your personal cost of living expenses and finances.

Other third level reflections include researching permits, licenses, insurance, making a marketing plan, financial forecasting, identifying and evaluating the facility, staff and equine requirements. These topics are specific enough that they each have their own chapter. So you might want to skip ahead to them after you have reviewed what is in a business plan so that you can give them the attention they need.

FIRST LEVEL REFLECTIONS

Find a quiet place to do these reflections. Track your thoughts in a way that works best for you. You can type directly into your computer, write notes in a journal, or record your thinking-out-loud comments. Choose the method that will help you let your mind flow. You are going to reflect on three layers–self, other, world. First ask yourself the following important questions about how your vision/business relates to you. Second, proceed to answer the questions about how your vision/business relates to others. And third, answer the questions on how your vision/ business relates to the world to large.

Once you have done this important first step, you may not need to repeat this for a very long time. But it is important to spend the time to reflect on these first level questions, as they are a hint to your deeper, often subconscious intentions, and desires that are pushing you to extend yourself into the world this way.

You can simplify this phase by thinking in terms of who, what, where, when, why, and how. Sometimes this creates a container for ease of thinking, but if it is confusing don't fuss over it. Don't suffer with this. Try to find the answers that flow and notice the areas that are difficult. This part of the process is for your personal clarity. Parts of your answers may or may not become part of your business plan.

ORGANIZE YOUR THOUGHTS INTO THREE LEVELS: SELF, OTHER, WORLD

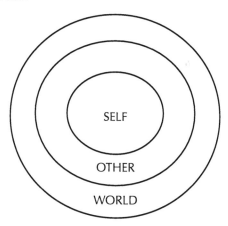

SELF

   1. WHO am I?
       a. What do I do best?
       b. Am I a self-starter or do I need help initiating new things?
       c. Am I more of a lead mare, or do I like to work with someone else's direction?
       d. Do I like a lot of structure or do I like to create on the spot?
       e. Am I more of an assertive or passive type of person?

f.   What are five of my strengths?

g.   What are five of my self-limitations?

2.   WHAT am I about?
   a.   What are my core values and beliefs about life, people, and relationships?
   b.   What am I willing to do to make my vision happen?
   c.   What am I not willing to do to make my vision happen?
   d.   What makes me happy?
   e.   What offends me?
   f.   What are my desired goals or outcomes if my vision comes true?

3.   WHY do I want to do this work?
   a.   Why is my vision important to me?

4.   WHEN am I going to feel ready to start my business?
   a.   Am I looking for approval from someone and if so whom?
   b.   What do I need in order to get started?
   c.   What are my excuses for not getting started? Are they grounded?

5.   WHERE do I see myself fitting in?

6.   HOW will I know that I am succeeding
   a.   With my vision?
   b.   In my offer?
   c.   With my business?
      i.   How many customers?
      ii.   How much gross income per month and per year?

OTHER

1.   WHO will my business offer be valuable to?
   a.   Who are the kinds of people I want to work with?
   b.   Will I focus on youth, adults or a combination of the two?
   c.   Who are the people who will support my vision/business?

2. WHAT type of issues, themes, concepts, learning do I want to work with?
    a. Some ways to think about this question include:
        i. Do I want to focus on helping people heal past experiences
        ii. Or do I want to help people in transitions or with life purpose inquiries?
        iii. Do I want to help people have better relationships with their horses?
    b. What promises am I making to my customers?

3. WHY is my vision important to other people, like my future customers?

4. WHEN will I offer my services?
    a. Year round, seasonally?

5. WHERE will I find my customers?
    a. What are my existing resources for potential customers?

6. HOW do I want others to see
    a. Me?
    b. My offers?
    c. The business concept?

WORLD

1. WHO will benefit most from my vision/business?
2. WHAT will be different in the world if my business is successful?
3. WHY is my vision important to the world?
4. HOW will the world be a different place if my vision/business succeeds?

SECOND LEVEL REFLECTIONS

After you have completed the first level reflections, use your responses to make a vision, mission, and purpose statement.

VISION

What do you see possible in the world? Your vision statement is a panoramic view that encompasses your deep-seated beliefs and values, goals and ambitions for the world at large. Your vision may be so big that it won't come to fruition in your lifetime. It is bigger than you and what you might actually achieve in your lifetime. Your vision is the overriding goal that your values, ethics and beliefs center around. It is what you spend a lifetime working towards. Create at least one paragraph and then distill it down to one sentence.

MISSION

Your mission is your personal statement about what you are committing yourself to accomplish in this lifetime. It reflects what you are about at a core level and what people can depend on you for. It is the organizing principle of your work and ultimately your business goals. Your mission includes what you want to be known for in your lifetime. Create at least one paragraph and then distill it down to one sentence.

PURPOSE STATEMENT

Your statement is your plan of action. It is what you are promising to do, what you are 'going to make happen'. It details how you plan to go about accomplishing your goals. It includes a timeline that can range from what you will do in the next six months to what you will do in the next one, three, five and ten years. It can include specifics like, how many people you plan to work with, how many horses you will have, where you will live, how much money you will make, etc.

Now you are ready to compile your business plan based on these reflections. The next chapter includes a sample of a business plan that you can modify to prepare your strategic plan, and create a document that you can share with partners, potential employees, etc. if you plan to ask for money or loans, you should refer to a more detailed business plan to be sure your plan has the professional quality it needs for financial institutions.

THIRD LEVEL REFLECTIONS

Third level reflections are like the nuts and bolts of your plans for your future. They include your business's vision and mission, your curriculum vitae and your personal and business financial forecasts. At the beginning of each year (just like I review my personal and professional goals) I review these items. I recommend that you do the same.

BUSINESS VISION, MISSION AND STATEMENT

Now that you have a good understanding of your personal motivations and deep desires to contribute to the greater good, go through the first and second level reflections from a business perspective. Go through the three levels of self (the business), others (the clients), and the world (the community). This phase of your thinking will inform and help you answer many of the questions that you need to answer in the business plan. You might want to review the questions that you need to answer in your business plan as mentioned in the next chapter before proceeding with this step. Some of the questions below can help your thinking.

THE BUSINESS SELF

1. WHO will be part of the business?
   a. Who makes up the business?
   b. What staff requirements will it need?
   c. What are five strengths the business wants to embody?
   d. What limitations need to be paid attention to?
   e. How will my strengths and limitations potentially influence the operation of the business? What are some practices I can engage in or resources from others to balance these potential influences?

2. WHAT are the core values and beliefs of the business?
   a. What is the spirit or energy of the business?

3. WHY and HOW is this business important to
   a. My community?
   b. My customers?
   c. The world at large?

4. WHEN will the business begin?
   a. What organizational structure will be needed to get it started?
   b. When will the business offer its services, seasonally, year round?

5. WHERE will the business make its offer?

6. HOW will I know that the business is succeeding
   a. With its vision?
   b. With its offers?
   c. With its customers?

OTHER

1. WHO will the business offer be of value to?
   a. Who are the kinds of people it will work with?
   b. Will it focus on youth, adults or a combination of the two?
   c. Who are the people who will support or be a resource for the business?
   d. Who will the business be marketed to?

2. WHAT type of issues, themes, concepts, learning will it specialize in?
   a. What promises does it make to my customers?
   b. What kind of results does it produce for customers?

WORLD

1. WHO will benefit most from the business?

2. WHAT will be different in the world if the business is successful?
3. HOW will the world be a different place if the business succeeds?

CURRICULUM VITAE

Your curriculum vitae is like a log or diary of all of your professional experiences. It is a historical accounting of your schooling, additional education (such as training programs), articles you may have written, talks you've given, etc. It's often recorded by date of accomplishment. If you do not keep track of your accomplishments, you might forget how much you've actually done. And it may come in handy when a potential client wants to know more details about your experience and knowledge.

PERSONAL FINANCIAL EVALUATION

Having a good working knowledge of your personal and business financial requirements is invaluable. Financial analysis gives you clear parameters so that you can make well thought out decisions about your business. Your personal financial requirements will help you to ground your thinking about how to start your business. It gives you a framework of what the minimum amount of money you need to generate in order to support you and your way of life. It will tell you if you can afford to focus solely on developing your new business or if you need to develop it in stages while maintaining other sources of income. It is an essential business practice.

In this section let's focus on your personal cost of living expenses. Sometimes it is helpful to do two versions. One is the 'bare bones' minimum amount of money you need to get by. The second is your 'ideal' cost of living. It's a good idea to do each forecast by the month and by the year. You can do this pre-budget analysis in Microsoft Excel so that you can set up columns for both the 'bare bones' version and the 'ideal' version. You can then choose the scenario that feels most comfortable for you. Once you feel pretty good about your personal financial requirements, you can make a budget in QuickBooks or other finance program.

This phase of evaluating your finances should be practical and not idealistic. Be conservative in predicting your capital requirements, timelines, sales and profits. Make it a practice to review it monthly, quarterly and annually. The chapter on "Finances" will cover your business overhead costs and Profit and Loss Statement, which is an important way to evaluate your business from a financial perspective.

SAMPLE OF COST OF LIVING EXPENSES

Auto
    Gas
    Loan payments
    Registration
    Repairs
Bank service charges
Clothing
Dining out
Donations and contributions
Education
Food
Garbage
Garden
Gifts
Health
    Beauty supplies, haircuts,
    nails, etc
    Gym
    Dental
    Medical
Insurance
    Health
    Auto
    Home

Kids and their activities and education
Maintenance and repairs
Miscellaneous
Mortgages or Rent
    Property taxes
Office
    Phone
    Postage
    Computer
    Satellite or Cable
    Supplies
Pets
    Horses?
Professional fees (lawyers, accountants)
Recreational activities including movies
Vacations and travel
Taxes
    Federal
    State
Utilities
    Electric
    Gas
    Water (or well maintenance)
    Sewer (septic maintenance)

SAMPLE BUSINESS PLAN

COVER PAGE

The cover page should include the name of your business, location and date of document.

TABLE OF CONTENTS

PLAN SUMMARY

This is a one-paragraph summary of the purpose of the business plan. What is the goal of the business plan? Is the business plan detailing the goals and strategy required to start the business or is it forecasting a new direction or plans for growth of an existing business? Is the purpose of the plan to provide a road map, a one to five year projection of the businesses growth, financial needs, and/or specific issues that need to be addressed?

BUSINESS DESCRIPTION

VISION STATEMENT

Provide a one sentence statement of the overarching vision of business that connects to larger worldview.

MISSION STATEMENT

Provide a one sentence description of the current values and intent of the business and what it stands for in today's world.

PURPOSE STATEMENT

List the services and/or products the business is promising to provide.

BUSINESS DESCRIPTION

Describe the details of the business with a practical, yet inspiring description of services.

- Is it a sole proprietorship, a partnership or a corporation?
- Include hours and days of operation, location, etc.
- Describe the type of potential customers including age range, financial bracket, career, educational background, etc.
- Explain why this business is important.
  - ❖ Note any statistics that prove your point that this business is important.
- Describe the services that the business provides.
- If it is an existing business, describe its past successes and track record, what it is known for, etc.

TARGET MARKET

Describe your potential customers. Describe why customers need or want your service/products. Include their perceived needs or expectations. Describe how many customers you plan to serve: daily, weekly, monthly and/or yearly. Discuss in detail how you will gain access to potential customers and any other demographics that you think are important factors. This can be average age, sex, education, etc.

MARKETING PLAN

Describe how you plan to reach your customers. Provide details including type of promotional materials to be used, frequency of marketing material promotions, etc.

COMPETITION

Review businesses that are similar to yours. Describe what they offer, where they are located, how they price their offer, etc. Discuss what you

Ariana Strozzi

assess makes them successful. Discuss how your business is similar or different to your competition. Describe what makes you stand apart from your competition, what makes you unique.

OPERATING PROCEDURES

Describe what facilities you need to be successful. Be realistic. You can discuss what you would like to grow into, but be sure to describe current facilities including offices, stables, etc.

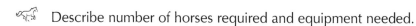

- Describe number of horses required and equipment needed.
- Provide a list as a separate appendix of items you have already acquired.
- Describe any issues or concerns that you have regarding facility, horses, and equipment needs that could cause unexpected obstacles to your success.
- Describe the kinds of licenses, permits, insurance you need or have and how you plan to address these topics.

PERSONNEL

Describe your personnel requirements. If you do not have all the skill sets required to make your business viable, discuss how you plan to compensate through hiring other staff or contracting with independent contractors.

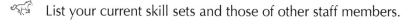

- List your current skill sets and those of other staff members.
- Discuss how your prior experiences apply to your business.
- Prepare and provide an appendix of your curriculum vitae and those of any personnel you may be hiring.

POTENTIAL CHALLENGES

Reflect on and discuss any potential obstacles, challenges or weaknesses you can. Discuss how you plan to address them.

FINANCIAL FORECASTS

Provide a summary of your financial forecasts for the company. Include what kind of funds or financial resources, working capital you need and or have to get started. If you do not have working capital (existing funds) describe how you plan to get it. Describe which services/products will produce what percent of overall gross income.

- Estimate percent of increase in gross revenues (income) you expect per quarter and/or per year. Discuss how this increase will occur. Be specific in terms of increase in number of customers, etc.

- Estimate percent of increase in expenses per quarter and/or per year as the business grows.

- Project what your net profit will be and what your assumptions are based on.

- Provide a balance sheet of current assets and liabilities as an appendix document.

- Provide a projected budget as an additional appendix document.

- Provide a Profit and Loss statement for current year and for one year out as an additional appendix document. You can also provide a review of previous year Profit and Loss statements to show trends of your business.

- Provide a list of fixed assets as an additional appendix item.

SUPPORTING DOCUMENTS

Supporting documents can be any additional information that you would like to include that has informed your business plan. If the business plan is for your internal use, you might want to include your earlier first and second level reflections. You might not want to list all of the competition statistics in your summary on competition so create an appendix for the additional information that you would like to have on hand to review if necessary. You may want to include an appendix of other research that you have used to ground your assumptions.

- Appendix A-Curriculum Vitae
- Appendix B- List of Current and/or Past Customers
- Appendix C-List of Competitors
- Appendix D-Balance Sheet
- Appendix E-Projected Budget
- Appendix F-Projected Profit and Loss Statement
- Appendix G- List of Current Assets
- Appendix H-List of Additional Equipment Needed and Associated Costs

ADDITIONAL RESOURCES

- sba.gov.bplans.com
- startupepa.org
- microsoft.com/smallbusiness/startuptoolkit
- myownbusiness.org

PERMITS, INSURANCE AND LICENSES

SOLE PROPRIETOR, PARTNERSHIP OR CORPORATION

Hire a business lawyer and a CPA that are familiar with ranch/farm related businesses to help you determine what type of business will best serve you. You will also be asking their advise on several other issues mentioned in this chapter. Keep them up to date and informed as you develop and grow your business, so that they can best serve you.

USE PERMITS

Use permits are associated with the physical address of your business and are very important considerations. Go to your local county planning department with your property's APN (parcel #) and find out what the zoning is and what the zoning allows. Find out what the fees for a use permit are and what the building codes, septic and well requirements are. Try to inform yourself of any hidden costs or fees. Some zoning laws may limit the number of horses you can have, etc. Zoning laws vary widely from county to county; so do not make any assumptions. Get informed.

CITY, COUNTY BUSINESS LICENSES

Depending on the location of your business, you may be required to get a business license or permit within your city or county. Go to your local city hall and county administration to determine if you need any permits or licenses in your area.

SELLER'S PERMIT

A seller's permit may or may not prove useful for your business. A seller's permit allows you to sell products like books and DVDs, art or other goods. It also allows you to buy merchandise at wholesale that you will be reselling. Go to your state board of equalization to determine if you want to get a seller's permit.

FICTITIOUS BUSINESS NAME STATEMENT

You will need a fictitious business name statement to open a business checking account. Go to your county administrative offices to complete your paperwork. This is a very inexpensive procedure usually costing less than $100. You will need to list all of the owners and the type of business (sole proprietor, partnership, corporation).

WORKERS COMPENSATION INSURANCE

If you plan to have employees you will need workers compensation insurance. Worker's compensation can be astronomical for employees who work around horses, so find out what you will expect to pay before you determine a pay rate for employees. You will also want to break out what percent of time employees spend with horses versus office or ground maintenance, because the workers compensation insurance will be a different rate per hour for each duty. Workers compensation insurance is an employment expense in addition to wages and associated employment taxes.

You should discuss with both your lawyer and accountant the pros and cons to hiring independent contractors versus employees. Your insurance agent may be able to help you secure workers compensation insurance or you can visit workerscompensation.com for more information.

EMPLOYEE SAFETY AND HEALTH REGULATIONS

If you plan to have employees you need to find out what the laws are in your state regarding employees. Your lawyer may be able to assist you with this.

INSURANCE

Insurance is a necessity. Liability issues and laws vary widely from state to state. Show your lawyer your business plan and ask him/her what they recommend in terms of insurance and release of liabilities. Do not copy someone else's release of liability, or modify one on your own. Your lawyer will need to feel comfortable defending you and any release form you use, so let him/her advise you to how he/she recommends that you proceed.

SOME INSURANCE RESOURCES INCLUDE:

LarryViegasInsurance.com
www.narha.org/SecEFMHA/EFMHInsuranceChecklist.asp
http://www.eagala.org/insurance.htm

TAXES

Have your accountant advise you on best business practices for your area and to determine how and when to pay your local, state and federal taxes.

FINANCES

Good financial practices are essential to running a successful business. If you are not experienced in financial practices, hire a qualified bookkeeper and CPA to assist you in setting up your financial tracking system. You want to set up your books so that you can track specific income and expenses on a profit and loss statement (P&L), assets and liabilities on a balance sheet, compare budget to actual, and compare current year income and expenses to previous years. It's best to use a financial program like QuickBooks that provides professional accounting software.

Set up separate accounts for your business finances and your personal finances. Categorize the types of income you plan to receive. For example, I separate private clinics from pubic clinics. Private clinics are those that are custom designed for specific teams or groups of people, distinct from public clinics that are advertised on the website and anyone can sign up for. Since I offer more than one type of public program, I have them listed as a sub-category of public programs, so I can look at the public programs overall or per type of program. I also have separate categories for my one on one coaching work, horse training, riding lessons, etc. Then, I have a separate category for books and DVDs, art, and product sales. By categorizing my income types, I am able to review what percent of each type of income contributes to the overall gross income.

My P&L is fairly detailed because I like to know exactly where my money comes from and where it goes. I like to be able to see at a glance how much I spend on feed for the horses distinct from feed for the sheep, so I have a separate line item for each. A sample P&L is listed at the end of this chapter. Before you create your P&L think about how you want to categorize your income in a way that is easy for you to understand and evaluate your finances. If you need help, give us a call and we can set you up with an appropriate financial coach.

DETERMINE YOUR OVERHEAD COSTS

Using your profit and loss statement and budget, estimate what your hard costs are to keep your doors open. This includes essential items you have to have in order to do business. Hard costs include the following expenses: phone, Internet, gas, electricity, rent, water, salary (which you need to cover your personal expenses), etc. Take the sum total of your hard costs (aka. overhead costs) and then break it down into per day, per week and per month values. This will give you a very quick idea of your daily overhead and will help you when it comes time to price your offer and estimate how many services you need to provide monthly and yearly to stay afloat. I recommend using Microsoft Excel for this project.

As I mentioned before you should keep your personal finances and your business finances separate. First complete your personal financial forecast, as discussed in the chapter on "Preparing Your Business Plan." Determine your monthly salary or wage that you need to maintain your personal finances. You can then plug that into your business budget/P&L as a line item called 'salary'. Once you have looked at your income and expenses from this perspective, you might need to go back and revise your budget and P&L forecast. Below are some examples of financial forecasting.

EXAMPLE 1:

Marsha has an existing practice as a life coach. She offers 1-1 sessions for her customers. She owns two horses and boards them at a local ranch. She rents part of the facility for her EGE work. She has determined that she will charge $150 per one-hour session. She breaks down her overhead costs as such:

BUSINESS OVERHEAD EXPENSES	PER YEAR	PER MONTH	PER WEEK	PER DAY (5day work week)
Phone	$1200	$100	$25	$5
Internet	$600	$50	$12.5	2.5

Office/computer	$480	$40	$10	$2
Facility rent	$6000	$500	$125	$25
Horse expenses: (Board, feed, veterinary care, hooves, etc)	$9000	$750	$187.5	$37.5
Insurance	$2500	$208	$52	$10
Marketing/Web PR	$5000	$465	$104	$21
Professional fees: (Lawyer, accountant)	$600	$50	$12.5	$2.5
SUBTOTAL	$25,380.00	$2,163.00	$528.50	$105.50
My Salary=personal expenses	$60,000	$5,000	$1,250	$250
TOTAL EXPENSES	$85,380.00	$7,163.00	$1,778.50	$355.50

By estimating her overhead and living expenses and breaking them down like this, Marcia is able to determine that she needs to make $355 per day or $1778 per week. This means that she needs to have twelve clients per week, or an average of three per day, at $150 per hour just to cover her personal and business expenses.

EXAMPLE 2:

Sally is a business coach and plans to provide private and public EGE programs between the months of May and October at the ranch she owns. She has four horses. She has not yet determined her staffing needs, and she manages the ranch on her own. She currently works as a consultant full-time and generates $135,000 salary per year. She wants to cut back to half time with a salary of $50,000 so that she can start her EGE business.

OVERHEAD EXPENSES	PER YEAR	PER MONTH	PER WEEK	PER DAY
Phone	$1,200	$100	$25	$5
Internet	$600	$50	$12.5	2.5
Office supplies	$480	$40	$10	$2
Mortgage, Property Tax	$48,000	$4,000	$1,000	$200
Horse expense (Feed, veterinary care, hooves, etc)	$7,200	$600	$150	$30
Insurance	$4,000	$333	$83	$17
Marketing/Web PR	$5000	$465	$104	$21
Professional fees (Lawyer, accountant)	$1,000	$83	$21	$4
Ranch maintenance (Septic, well, fences, etc.)	$15,000	$1,250	$312	$78
Utilities	$7,200	$600	$150	$30
SUBTOTAL	$89,680.00	$7,521.00	$1,867.50	$389.50
My Salary=personal expenses	$36,000	$3,000	$750	$150
TOTAL EXPENSES	$125,680.00	$10,473.00	$2,618.00	$523.00

Sally's monthly expenses are much higher than Marcia's because she owns the ranch and the cost of maintenance and insurance is much higher. She is planning on offering a three-day public program every six weeks for a total of four programs between May and October, (she is hesitant to consider the other months because of potentially bad weather and since the participants come from far away locations, she cannot cancel the programs if the weather is bad). She also estimates that her existing network and marketing base would allow one program every six weeks, which only allows four programs in the six-month window of May-October. Her first projection is for ten participants paying $650 each.

Option 1:
10 participants/program x **$650** g. income/participant = $6500 g. income per program
4 programs x $6500 g. income/program = $26,000
Projected Income from consulting work = $50,000
$50,000 + $26,000 = $76,000 gross income for EGE and consulting work
Short by $50,000

Option 2:
10 participants/program x **$650** g. income/participant = $6500 g. income per program
10 programs x $6500 g. income/program =$65,000
Projected Income from consulting work = $50,000
$50,000 + $65,000 = $110,000 gross income for EGE and consulting work.
Short by $16,000.

Option 3:
10 participants/program x **$950** g. income/participant = $9,500 g. income per program
6 programs x $9500 g. income/program = $57,000
Projected Income from consulting work = $50,000
$50,000 + $57,000 = $107,000 gross income for EGE and consulting work
Short by $19,000

Option 4:
10 participants/program x **$950** g. income/participant = $9,500 g. income per program
8 programs x $9500 g. income/program = $76,000
Projected Income from consulting work = $50,000
$50,000 + 76,000 = $126,000 gross income for EGE and consulting work

By taking the time to do her financial projections, she realizes that her original projections of four programs at $650 per participant will not cover her expenses. She considers option 2: ten programs generating $6,500 each. Even if she were to achieve this lofty goal, 10 programs only provide her with $65,000 in income towards $125,680 in expenses. A part-time salary of $50,000 per year and her projected income of $65,000 will still leave her short by $16,000.00.

Another option is to raise her tuition per participant. If she raises the program tuition to $950 per participant, her gross income per program would be $9500. 10 programs at $9500 gross income per program would be $75,000 and would cover her expenses.

She asks herself if ten programs in a six-month period is a reasonable projection. Ten programs in six months is an average of one program every two and a half weeks. That seems like a lot to start off with. She reviews her database of potential clients. If she were to do ten programs per year, she would require a total of 100 participants (10 per program). How many prospects would she need to have in her database to get that many participants? Probably 2,000-5,000. And she only has 300. So, even her idea of doing ten programs in six months is overly optimistic and ultimately unrealistic. And she hasn't even included staff needs, course expenses, etc.

Because she has done her financial forecasting she realizes that she needs to keep her full time consulting position while she test pilots her public programs. Yes, she will be working more than full-time for a while, but with the additional expenses of the ranch, it is her most practical option. She is now able to forecast growing into her business over a two to three year period and promises to herself to grow her business to her projections over a two year period, at which time she can cut back to part-time consulting.

PRICING YOUR OFFER

As you can see from the previous examples, knowing your cost of living and overhead expenses is important knowledge to have before you make final decisions on how to price your services. In addition to financial projections, you need to do some market research of what other professionals in the field and similar fields are charging. What are other therapists and coaches charging for one on one sessions, for group sessions and for public programs?

If you are planning on doing public programs look into what other educational programs that teach similar subject matter are charging per day. Be sure to look at the details of their program. A lot of programs are listed as three-day programs, but they start in the evening of day one and are only in session for two to three hours. Day two is a full day, and day three is three hours (only half a day). In my opinion, that is not really a three-day program, it's more like a two-day program. If your three-day program is three full days you may need to price your program differently.

Next evaluate your actual costs to put on a program. For example, you plan to offer a three-day public program. What is the minimum number of participants you need to have in the program to make it viable for you? What are the costs of staff, food, snacks, written materials? What are your daily and/or weekly overhead costs?

Evaluate the range of costs with your income requirements and come up with a happy medium. You may decide that your services are a high-end offer, in which case you would price your offers on the high side. Be sure not to undercharge for your services, as people will wonder what is wrong with your offer. I've seen many new offers in this profession with prices that are too low. It looks like a giveaway, or creates an implied statement like, "I'm just getting started and not sure of my offer, so I am offering it for cheap (because maybe that is what it is worth?)."

MONTHLY, QUARTERLY AND YEARLY REVIEWS

Best practices include reviewing your financial books at the end of each month, each quarter and each year. I review my P&L and compare it to the previous year at the end of every month. This gives me a sense of what months are high-income months, and what months are low-income months. It helps me adjust my future budget and end of the year tax impact. It also tells me if I need to focus more attention on marketing, selling and promoting my business.

At the end of each year review each source of income and determine what percent of total income it makes up. You might find over time that some of your services are in far more demand than others. For example, you might find that your private coaching is far more profitable than doing public programs or vice versa. The market will start to tell you where your gift actually is- if you listen to it. Reviewing your finances along with your business plan at the end of each year will help you to make informed decisions about your future projections and goals. It will also ease your worries. You will either know that your business is doing well financially or it is not. And if it is not, at least you know it and can make some decisions to change its financial status.

If you need any assistance with the financial practices discussed in this chapter, you can contact our offices for coaching services to help you get set up.

EXAMPLE OF A PROFIT AND LOSS STATEMENT

GROSS Income
- Programs
    - 08-Public Programs
    - 08-Private Programs
- Private Coaching
- Boarding
- Riding Lessons
- Horse Training
- Facility Rental
- Reimbursed expenses

TOTAL GROSS INCOME

EXPENSES

Administration (hard costs)
- Office
    - Computer Repairs
    - Internet
    - Phone
    - Postage
    - Website Maintenance
    - Payroll/Salary
- Advertising
- Bank Service Charges
- Business Entertainment
- Contributions
- Dues and Subscriptions
- Education

Equine Maintenance
- Feed
- Hooves and worming
- Veterinary care

Facility
- Maintenance and Repairs
    - Equipment Repair
    - Gas
    - Garbage
    - Porta potty
    - Rent

Insurance

Miscellaneous

Professional fees
- Lawyer
- Accountant
- Other advisors

Program expense
- Food
- Handouts

Supplies
- Tack
- Uniforms

Taxes

Travel

TOTAL EXPENSES

NET INCOME (gross income minus expenses)

MARKETING

KNOWING YOUR MARKET

Marketing addresses how you promote your business and how you plan to reach your targeted audience. Marketing materials include websites, advertisements in magazines and newspapers, postcards, flyers, brochures, e-newsletters, etc. It will be important to develop a strategy for reaching your customers through your marketing materials on an ongoing basis.

An important step before making your marketing plan is to define your niche. Your niche is comprised of your specialty (what type of work you plan to do) and the type of people you plan to work with. Your market niche may also be determined by your location. If you plan on doing 1-1 work, then you need to make sure that the types of people you want to work with live near your physical location. It may be influenced by the seasons and weather conditions. It may be influenced by other recreational activities in the area, local accommodations, and other resources that either you or your customers need in order to engage together.

Some EGE professionals are highly specialized. For example, some professionals only work with health professionals such as doctors and hospital administrators. Most often this is because they have expertise in this domain and know what their potential customers issues, breakdowns and opportunities are. Their existing competency in a specific domain allows them to understand and relate directly to their customers' concerns. They also have existing networks of peers and colleagues who can act as referral sources.

Some professionals plan to work with women who have experienced trauma because it is an area that they have specific interest and knowledge in. Others work with a broad spectrum of people from various professions, locations and financial status.

A fancy website, beautiful brochures and colorful business cards are not going to bring in customers. They may attract their attention. But if your message is unclear or confusing they will grow disinterested as fast as their head can turn in another direction. Your knowledge of the needs of your potential customers and how your service can take care of them will allow you to focus your website, promotional material and written content directly towards your targeted customer.

Bear in mind that EGE and any form of 'Horse as Healer/Teacher' service is a very new offer in the marketplace. The majority of your potential customers are not even aware that such a service exists. The concept that horses can be teachers and healers may be so foreign that they find your offer to be entirely confusing and discount it before really looking into it. If this is the case, they will need to be EDUCATED about why your offer is important to them. This means that you really need to know 'who' they are and 'what' their concerns are and how your offer directly relates to their issues. You have to be able to 'speak into their listening'. If you just speak about you and how cool your offer is and how wonderful the horses are (and so on and so on), they might think it is interesting, but they probably won't enroll. On the other hand, if you explain how your work will benefit them by explaining the types of results you produce, you have a better chance of capturing their interest.

Right now, in today's market, the only people that really understand your offer might be other professionals in the field. And even then, the potential for doubt and confusion is rampant because there are so many acronyms and splintering of offers. Our general lack of alignment as an industry does indeed have an impact on all of our ability to close the sale on our services. As a result, we have to literally assume that our potential customers know nothing about EGE or EAP or EFL, etc.

Therefore, take the time to really think through your offer, and what it can promise to your customer base. Explain clearly and concisely what your offer is and how it can help your customers. You will need to know the demographics of your customer base in order to direct your marketing plan specifically to them. If you have not already done so, review some of the questions in the "Preparing a Business Plan" chapter to gain clarity on your offer and why your customers need it. Spend some quality time reflecting on the specific types of people you plan to work with. Maybe even go out an interview them, to hear their opinions. This is a very important step in planning your business and will become part of your business plan. Once you have gained clarity about the needs and demographics of your potential customers, you will be able to make informed decisions about where and how to spend your dollars on marketing strategies.

Below I have offered a few questions to spur your thinking.

DEMOGRAPHICS OF YOUR POTENTIAL CUSTOMER BASE

- What is their age range?

- What is their financial status?

- What is their educational background?

- Do they have the decision making power to sign up for your offer. If not, who has decision-making power on their behalf? This is especially important when you are working with companies or teams.

- What are their career demographics? How do they utilize their intellect? Are they used to hotel conference rooms? How do they communicate with their network?

- Does religion influence them?

- Are they located in proximity to your facility or will they have to travel to reach you?

- What are some of the recurrent issues they face?

- Do they have the resources of time, money and transportation to accept your offer?

- Will they be able to understand and relate to your offer or will you have to educate them as to why your service is valuable?

- Why does this specific audience need your service?

- What publications do they read?

🐎 What trade shows do they go to?

🐎 What do they spend the majority of their time doing? What do they do when they are not working?

🐎 What's your sense of their value or belief system?

HOW YOUR BUSINESS WILL SERVE YOUR CUSTOMERS

🐎 How will your offer address this audience?

🐎 What do you promise to offer to them?

🐎 What are specific results you can promise they will achieve through your work?

🐎 What challenges may you need to overcome to market your service/products to them?

🐎 How will your specific facilitation style complement your offer to your potential customers?

🐎 What distinguishes you from other offers?

🐎 Is weather and season an issue for your customers?

🐎 How is your physical facility located in relation to your customers? Will they need lodging? Will they need restaurants or markets?

MARKETING OPTIONS

🐎 Local newspaper advertisements: Fairly inexpensive way to get exposure for your business. Do not expect much response. But you can start to gain name recognition for your business. If you are going to pay for advertising in newspapers, magazines, journals, plan to repeat your ad up to six times or more. One-time ads have very low impact.

🐎 Local magazine advertisements: Try to target your audience by choosing a magazine that they read. Magazine ads can be pricey and not very effective, but it might be worth trying if you can find a specific magazine that targets the same audience as you. If you are going to pay for advertising in newspapers, magazines, journals, plan to repeat your ad up to six times or more. One-time ads have very low impact.

🐎 Classified Ads: A cheap way to experiment with reaching potential customers.

🐎 Website: The public generally expects any business to have a website. And for that reason alone it is an important marketing tool. It may or may not lead to actual sales. Refer to a web expert on this topic. You may receive numerous inquiries via the Internet, but these may not lead to actual sales.

🐎 Brochures: Used to be necessary, but not necessary in today's market. They are nice to have to hand out or direct mail.

🐎 Direct Mail: Brochures, postcards and flyers are a relatively effective way to reach your market. Requires that you build a database of potential customers, which is discussed in the chapter on Administrative Notes.

🐎 Introductory offers: One way to educate and expose potential customers to the value of your offer. Options include two to four hour or one-day introductory programs. I've found it hard to do short introductions. One reason for this is that I find it hard to draw a boundary between offering a general introduction and really getting into the potential of the work. I also find it hard to expose the public to the horses without having the time to build the context and some basic principles to study. Now, that could just be me. I observe that some new professionals in the field utilize this form of marketing quite a bit. It may be worth trying out and see if you think it is a good way to market yourself and your program. In order to do this well, you will need to have a very clear idea of the topics you want to cover and the exercises you want to provide.

🐎 Word of Mouth Referrals: The best form of marketing. These potential clients have either noticed someone they care about change because of working with you, or they have been told how great your service is. Treat them personally. Find out who recommended them and why. Word of mouth referrals do not cost any marketing dollars and are practically ready to accept your offer. Focus on these prospects as much as possible. Make them a priority in your marketing plan.

- Articles: Writing articles for trade magazines are a great way to get the word out about your offer. Remember that most of the people reading it will be other professionals. You will gain name recognition among your peers, but may not lead to actual new customers. You can use the articles to hand out to potential customers. If they know your peers respect you, they will be more likely to accept your offer. It is also good to document these in your curriculum vitae.

- Direct contact: Perhaps the best marketing strategy is finding direct contact to your customers. Look for opportunities to set up appointments with potential customers. Timely responses to customer inquiries are essential. It sounds obvious, but consistent, reliable follow through builds customer satisfaction.

- Creating networks and alliances: Other professionals who may be in potentially competitive markets may actually be resources for you. For, example, Jane in North Carolina receives a call from a potential customer in Washington State who requests her services. She knows she cannot deliver, but she can refer her to a colleague, Sue, who she studied with in the EGE certification program. If Jane establishes a referral system with Sue, she can receive a referral fee, and Sue will be more likely to refer her to someone on the East Coast.

Another example of network building is creating an alliance with a neighboring hotel or spa. You refer your customers to them for lodging and they refer their customers to your educational offers. I'll share another example at the end of this chapter of reciprocal competition and its benefits.

EDUCATING POTENTIAL CUSTOMERS IS A FORM OF STORYTELLING

I mentioned earlier that you might need to educate your potential customers about the value of your offer because the concept of 'Horse as Healer/Teacher' is still so new. Educating your customers means that in your promotional material you need to explain why your offer is so important. Whether you are speaking conversationally or writing text, avoid detailing the process itself. Rather, tell a story. Tell an actual event that you think the person you are trying to reach can resonate with.

For example, tell how Joe (you may not want to say his name for confidential reasons), a finance executive, came out to work with the horse. He was having problems with (x) or was in (y) transition/dilemma, and when he had his session with the horse he realized (a). Through this amazing insight, he was able to make the big decision to change (b) and now he is doing (c).

You may share your own personal experience of how you decided to do this work in the first place. You might share personal accounts of how impactful this work has been on you as an individual and as a professional. I've always been deeply moved when I hear many of the EGE professionals' stories of how they came to doing this work. I notice a beginning level of trust is built by adding this personal dimension. It helps potential customers begin to bond with you and understand more about you and why you are doing this work.

After a brief period of storytelling, make promises that you can produce specific results that you have estimated your potential customers are looking for. Be clear and concise. Do not be afraid of being too specific. It's better to be too specific than to be all over the place.

TIPS

- Avoid offering too many services. Especially when you are just starting out, focus on one specific offer to a specific audience.

- Don't try to be everything for everybody.

- Avoid promising services that you cannot deliver on.

Do not offer your services for less than the going rate. Potential customers will sense that you are not confident in your offer. They will wonder why you are so cheap.

 Choose and stick with one to three typefaces, sizes and styles to be used in all of your promotional material.

 Choose and stick with a color scheme. Use these colors consistently.

 Mass advertising is generally ineffective. Consider that out of a mailing to 1000 addresses, you can expect 1-2% sales. Remember that inquiries are not sales.

 Be specific. Offer specific dates and times that people can accept your offer. Avoid offering public programs or services that do not have specific dates and costs on your advertising materials. You may lose some potential customers because they do not want to take the extra time to call you to find out the dates and times.

 Avoid negativity and judgmental language in your promotional material. Remember you are trying to offer an opportunity that should sound optimistic.

 Have a friend or colleague review your marketing material before you make it public.

 Ask people how they found out about you. This way you will learn what marketing strategies you employed are actually working for you.

 Track which marketing strategies are effective by doing statistics on % of income in relation to cost of marketing. If you design your database to track 'how your customers found out about you', you can determine which advertising strategies are working and which are not. I will discuss database management in the next chapter.

 Review websites, advertisements and other marketing materials and ask yourself why you like them. What appeals to you? What does not? Is it the colors, the cleanliness of the design? Is it the clarity of their message?

- Determine your existing resources of potential customers. Who do you already know that your service might be useful to? What clubs, groups do you belong to that you could speak at or network at? What friends, family, and community resources can you utilize? Your existing resources are your most important and inexpensive resources.

- Identify other potentially competitive offers and see if you can create a network alliance.

- Send thank you notes and acknowledge people who you notice refer business to you.

- If you have a hard time writing about or promoting yourself, pretend you are someone else writing about you or ask someone else to write about you.

WHAT HAS WORKED BEST FOR ME

The majority of my business comes from word of mouth and referral. I find that this is the most effective form of marketing. My best customers have always found me through a previous customer. At the same time, I acknowledge that it takes years to build this type of marketing. In the early years I did quite a bit of marketing via all of the above-mentioned ways. I kept good records in my database so that I was able to discern which marketing strategies worked over others.

I've learned that the sooner I can make contact via phone or person, the more likely I am to complete the sale. I have also learned that it is not nearly as effective to start the conversation (with a potential customer) by describing 'my' offer, but rather, to learn more about them first. I look for the first opportunity to ask them to tell me a bit more about them and what they are looking for. Once I know more about them, I can gear the description of my offer to show how it can benefit them specifically.

I learned that it's important to develop a consistent description of my offers. Too many different program names and descriptions create too much confusion in the potential customer. Also, too much description can overwhelm. I enjoy the challenge of trying to articulate the offer and its promises in as short a description as possible. Once I have the potential customers interest, I can go into further detail.

I place ads in local magazines to support them, and do not expect actual sales from the ad. I am clear that my investment in this form of advertising is to show that I am a member of the community and I am willing to support related endeavors of value. Sometimes this encourages 'trickle down' prospects.

I spend less than 5% of my gross revenues on marketing. I know from experience that it is entirely up to me to engage quickly and effectively with potential customers. Ads and promotional pieces do not make the sale. Running a ranch adds extra complexity because I am rarely by the phone. I think one of the best business practices is to pick up the phone in person, but it is one of the hardest practices for me to accomplish. I know I lose business over it.

I know I could invest in more staff support to accomplish more immediate customer service. I used to have staff that answered the phone, but over time I lost contact with my potential customers and that did not sit well with me. So I decided to go back to being more hands on in my business. Even though my business is smaller as a result, I am content with it the way it is. I do not want to maintain a lot of staff and so I make do the best I can with the resources I have.

Another successful marketing tool I use (when it is appropriate) is building alliances with other offers that are closely related to mine. For example, Rayona, the founder of Institute for Women's Leadership came through my program and was very interested in incorporating the Leadership & Horses™ program into her executive leader program. She was hesitant to commit to it because she wasn't sure what her customers would think. Would it be too 'out there' for them? After several circular conversations, I decided to offer a one-day program for her customers for no charge. I knew I could produce satisfaction, and if they liked it they would incorporate the horse work into the program.

She accepted my generous offer, and the day was so successful that she now incorporates the Leadership & Horses™ day into the beginning of her executive leader program. I work with her customers several times a year and have done so for over six years now. If I had not made that pro-bono offer, I never would have gotten in the door. When one of her customers wants to do additional work with me, I make sure that Rayona is agreeable (since this is her customer) and I pay her a percent of the income I receive.

ADMINISTRATION

OFFICE PRACTICES

Good office practices are a daily part of running a successful business. For the most part, I am going to assume that you already have pretty good office practices. Make your office a place that you enjoy being in. As a business owner you will need a quiet place to think, speculate and design your business. It never ceases to amaze me how much quiet, uninterrupted time I actually need to focus on the business.

Over the years, I have discovered that the kind of mental attention required for making financial forecasts, visioning the future of the business, making marketing decisions, and other business projections is very different than sitting behind a desk, organizing papers and answering the phone. In fact, I have learned that when I am doing these more heady tasks, I do not like to have a phone nearby, because it distracts me and pulls me out of a specific state of consciousness that is hard to recover when interrupted.

Explore what environment works best for you to talk to potential customers versus doing big picture thinking. What time of day is your most productive, focused period? For me it is in the morning before the unexpected distractions of the ranch start to pull my attention in a variety of directions. I begin my day by answering emails and phone calls. Then I spend up to a few hours on business details. If I meet someone in person I try to do it over a meal. Mid day I am usually out working with clients, horses or on the ranch. Sometimes I make calls in the late afternoon, but I know I cannot depend on that so I try to do all of my sales conversations before noon.

Everyone is different so find what patterns work best for you. Notice where you are pretty efficient and the areas where you need extra focus. I know the hardest thing for me to do is sit down and focus on phone calls and correspondence. Knowing that this is one of the most important parts of my job, I do it in the morning when I have the most focus. In this way, I am less likely to come up with excuses for why I need to be doing something else. Do the hard stuff (the stuff you like to do the least) first, then the easy stuff.

KEEPING TRACK OF YOUR CUSTOMERS

Creating a database that captures and retains valuable information on your customers is priceless. Do not skip over this practice. How you keep track of potential, existing and past customers is like having money in the bank. Your customers are your business. Without them, you do not have income. Keeping track of conversations with potential customers is time consuming, but well worth the effort. Good filing habits actually free up your time because when you need to find information quickly you know where it is.

It is very hard to go back after the fact and try to recover information because you didn't have a good database system in the first place. So take the time to think through what kind of information you want to have on hand about your customers.

The most common use of a database is to store addresses, phone numbers and email addresses so that you can send them information or correspond via phone or email. There is a lot more to database management than that. You might want to remember personal details about them like their spouses name or the names of their children. You might want to be able to keep track of the conversations and negotiations you had with them, or emails/letters you sent them or they sent you. You might want to keep track of what programs they took from you or summaries of your private sessions with them.

Information that you collect on past, present and future customers can also be used to create statistics. For example, what percent of your customers are male/female, married/divorced, etc. Consider what kinds of things you want to know about your market. Below are some things to consider keeping track of. I am going to focus on a database for an adult clientele. If you will be working with youth, you might want to add or delete some of the items. Also, if you are a therapist or social worker there might be other criteria that you want to cover as well.

Name

 Home address and/or business address, country

 Phone # (home and/or business), fax #

 Email address

 Website address

 Date of birth

 Age

 Sex

 Married, single

 # of kids, kids names, spouses name

 Notes

 Date of original inquiry

 Date work with client begins, date of completion

I designed my original database in Filemaker because it offered the most flexibility in data management. At one point in time, we had several staff people that needed to be in the database at the same time and we wanted to track detailed information on our customers. Filemaker allows multiple users, creates and keeps track of form letters, nametags, mailing labels, envelopes, etc. When it got too complicated for me to design the database to the next level, I hired an expert and spent a significant amount of money to have it do everything I wanted it to do.

I wanted to keep track of basic contact information. That's easy. All kinds of programs do this nowadays. However, a lot of the other programs do not track the other information that I also wanted to have available. I wanted to be able to mail out newsletters and other promotional materials to past, present and future customers, but I also wanted to mail out postcards for an annual picnic to local friends. So I had a category established where I could 'do a find' for just local friends, people interested in art, or my whole database. I also wanted to keep track of conversations I had with contacts and any information they provided me in their initial inquiry. I wanted to be able to make nametags, mailing labels, etc.

I wanted to know when potential customers first contacted me so that every couple of years I could purge my database and get rid of contacts that were not active and had not been active in years. However, I did not want to delete past customers. I also wanted to track what programs they attended. I designed my database to organize all of my public programs so that I could track potential participants. I could record when I received their registration form and their payment. I can go back and look at any past program and see who was in the class. Granted, it is time consuming to enter data into the program when a new contact is entered. But the time I spend is well worth the flexibility and versatility of the information I am able to retain.

You have alot of options. Before you decide on a database program, check out what Filemaker, Act, and Microsoft Office can do for you. You might even want to consider having your files in physical files systems. The method of database collection and storing will be largely determined by the kind of data you want to retain.

CHOOSING A FACILITY

You may be one of those folks who have your own facility. But if you are not, it is possible to find a public or private stable that you can rent or utilize to operate your business from.

Whether you are evaluating an existing location (to rent or own) or building your facility from the ground up, I have compiled some general notes to consider. The following notes are my general opinion and come from over 38 years of experience. You may find quite a variety of opinions in the horse world regarding some of the topics covered in this chapter. Therefore it is important for you to find your own comfort level with each of the following topics. Let's begin by reviewing some of the most important things to consider in finding a facility.

HOW DO YOU <u>FEEL</u> ABOUT THE PLACE?

Does your body relax when you arrive? Do you feel safe and nurtured? Or do you become tense and anxious? Answering this question is one of your most important pieces of information in deciding on a place. If you don't feel comfortable, trust your sensate response. I have heard many stories of a new rider who does not listen to her first impressions of a facility that she plans to ride horses at. On her initial visit to the facility, she noticed that all of the horses were tense, high strung and anxious. She felt mildly uncomfortable, but brushed it aside. During her second ride on a new horse in the arena, she again felt uncomfortable. She didn't say anything and began riding a horse she had hoped to sponsor. The horse became tense and started moving around the arena too quickly and she fell off breaking her back. She has fully recovered, but shares her story of the consequences of not listening to her early impressions of the facility.

People that live, recreate, and work at the facility can exude an energy that is either in harmony with the space or in disharmony. It could be one person, or a whole group of people. It is not that their 'bad' people, it is just that they can contribute a negative energetic alignment to the property, the horses and the land itself.

Different properties have different personalities, just like people and horses do. Land is like anything else that you form a relationship with. There is an energetic tone to the land, a destiny or spiritual purpose. It also holds a vast history of experiences, which may be completely unknown to you. The land will speak to you if you allow yourself to listen to it.

WEATHER CONSIDERATIONS

What are the weather patterns like in the area? Are there seasonal high winds? What direction do the winter storms come from? Is flooding a concern? How about standing water? If you are not familiar with the area, take the time to research the weather patterns as they change seasonally. I have seen many barns that were built without consideration to the weather only to have stall fronts or pasture overhangs facing into the direction of winter storms. This means that the areas intended to protect the horses will be inundated with rain and wind during winter storms defeating the purpose of the shelter in the first place not to mention, difficulties in feeding horses, keeping feed and bedding dry and moving horses in and out of stabled areas.

The direction of the wind changes with the season. Wind will not only blow bedding around making your barn dusty and messy, but it will also be uncomfortable to work in over long periods of time. Sometimes you can't avoid the wind, but get to know its seasonal directions so you can plan your use of the facility accordingly.

If you will be doing EGE or similar type work outside, knowing your weather patterns is important in terms of providing your customers with a reasonable place to learn outside. There is no way to avoid weather if you are going to work outside, but there are ways you can work with it (most of the time).

BARNS

The main purpose of barns varies greatly from place to place. Generally speaking, barns are used for hay, bedding and tack storage, grooming areas, and protection for horses to get out of the weather. You definitely need a dry place to store hay, feed and tack. It is nice to have a place to groom and handle horses inside when the weather is bad, but it is not a requirement. It is also important to have a quiet, dry place protected from the weather for horses that are sick or injured. Things to consider in evaluating a barn include:

🐎 What condition are the exterior walls are in? If the walls are wood, they will need regular maintenance of either painting or staining to maintain the life of the wood.

🐎 How are the stall doors made? I prefer stall doors that swing open versus sliders. I have seen a horse seriously injured in a sliding stall door accident in which she got her foot caught in the door when part of it fell off of its track.

🐎 Is there plenty of space to move horses in the breezeway area? For example, if a horse is tied in the barn and spooks will it have enough room to recover or is it in danger of falling into something that could injure it?

🐎 Does the barn have electricity? Electricity is not essential in a barn. If it does not have electricity, then you should have a generator on hand in case you ever need light at night or the vet needs it when they are caring for your horses.

🐎 Remember that horses can and will get out of their pastures and stalls and easily find their way through the barn. So it is important that grains and supplements be placed in areas that horses cannot get into if loose.

🐎 How is the plumbing in the barn? Is there a shut off valve in each stall and to the barn itself? Horses are notorious at breaking water pipes and automatic waterers, so be sure to design easy ways to shut off water for repairs.

While horses are quite rugged creatures, often preferring to stay in open spaces during inclement weather, many horse owners enjoy the feeling of providing shelter for them. Remember that horses are still hard wired to live on the plains and as such, may not feel comfortable in pasture shelters. They may feel compromised as if they are afraid that they cannot flee from danger if necessary. A good pasture shelter has an open feeling to it that allows a horse to feel like it can enter and exit with ease and not feel trapped. Don't get your feelings hurt if your horse does not use the fancy shelter you provide it.

PADDOCKS

In an ideal situation horses need outdoor spaces to graze, be with other horses and run. An ideal facility has both small paddock areas as well as large pastures. Not all facilities have enough land for large pastures, but a good minimum field would be at least an acre. Horses like to be with other horses. That is their nature. If you can stand it, let them pasture together as much as possible, preferably all of the time. Your horse will be happier and healthier-physically, emotionally and mentally. Some people prefer to keep geldings and mares separate. I don't. I try to let my horses be as close to a natural herd as possible, so I mix mares and geldings together. This is a matter of personal preference, so do what feels right for you.

Occasionally you will need to confine a horse to a smaller paddock in the event of an injury or illness. If a horse needs confinement due to a leg injury, a 12'x12' run is a good minimum size in addition to having a 24'x24' or 24'x48' paddock as the horse heals and can stand minor activity.

ARENAS AND ROUND PENS

What you will need in terms of work areas such as arenas and round pens will vary depending on your intended use and space availability of the facility. Will you be primarily working 1-1 with your customers? Will you want to do herd studies, herd dynamics, energy layer activities, and active exercises with horses? If you will only be working on an individual basis with customers, it might not be necessary to have an arena or round pen. You might be able to work in one of the paddocks. If this is the case, I recommend not having the horse work in its home environment. It is a good idea to distinguish areas at the facility from the horses' home, neutral spaces and working environment. If you do not have a round pen or arena, designate a work area, which could also serve as a turn out area.

Some professionals work with their customers in the horses' home pasture. If the pasture is quite large and the horse has the freedom to come and go, engage or retreat, then that is probably ok. But there are a few things to take into consideration. The most important concern is other horses. In a pasture environment, other horses can compete for attention, which can create an unsafe environment for you and your customer. It can become quite dangerous being in the midst of a group of horses who are negotiating with each other as they will often kick and bite at each other and you certainly would not want you or your customer to be caught in the middle of that. I would advise not to work in pastures with numerous horses unless you are an extremely seasoned horseperson, you know the horses very well and they do not compete for attention.

Another issue to keep an eye out for if you do decide to work in the horse's home space is to notice if the horse becomes agitated or irritated. He/she might be telling you that their home space is sacred space for them. In this case find another area to designate as work area.

If you plan to have your customers working with the horses in hand, you need to consider where you will do that. For example, if you will be outside around the barn and not in a fenced in area, you will want to make sure that the grounds are safe in case the horse gets loose. Is the property fenced so that the horse cannot get out on the road? Are the grounds relatively free of dangerous objects?

Round pens are not necessary, but have become quite popular in recent years. I would not advise a round pen that is smaller than a 40-foot diameter. Both horse and human need to have space to retreat if necessary. An ideal round pen is between 50-60 feet in diameter. If you plan to move the horse around for exercise, footing should also be considered. I would avoid round pens with enclosed sides. In the EGE work there are so many interesting opportunities that arise when the round pen has an open feel to it.

Arena size varies tremendously and is usually governed by the space available in relation to the property itself, the barn, pastures and paddocks. If you have lots of space and plan to build an arena, an 80'x180' arena is an optimal arena size. Your money will be well spent, as you will be able to do anything in that arena-EGE, herd dynamics, horse training. If you ever have to sell the property your investment will have been well spent, as most horse trainers will be looking for an arena of this size.

If you do not have the space for an arena of this size, then do the best you can. 80' is a good minimum width. Anything smaller than that gets a bit crampy when you are riding for sport or training. Try for a minimum of 100' for arena length if you can. At the very least your arena can be a place where your horses can run and stretch their legs. Also if you ever diversify or turn your barn into more of a recreational riding it will be important to have space to work the horses. As far as footing goes, check out your local options. I would avoid old-tire footing, because if there ever were a fire, that material is very flammable and toxic when burning.

FENCING

There is no such thing as perfect fencing material. All fencing has potentially dangerous aspects for horses. Fencing that is between horses is the most important fencing to consider. Horses that are separated by fencing will lean on fences, kick fences, rear up on fences, and generally try to remove them to get to the horse(s) on the other side. It is essential to check out the fencing provided at an existing facility or really think through how you want to design your fencing. If you will be putting in your own fencing, cost is also a consideration. Check out your local livestock supply stores as well as local hardware stores before making your fencing choices.

WOOD

Personally I love wood fencing. It is the least dangerous material and is aesthetically pleasing, and easy to repair. But horses like to chew wood. Some horses really, really like to chew wood, so much so that they can destroy your beautiful new fence in a matter of days. And wood boards can come off relatively easily when kicked by horses. If you really love wood, consider using it in low impact areas, i.e. fencing that is not separating horses from each other. Maybe your arena could be wood. Wood is also nice for perimeter fences in highly visible areas, such as near your horse or driveway. You can also string a hot wire on the top or mid-section of the wood fence so the horses do not chew on it or rub against it.

Also important to consider in wood fencing if it is pressure treated wood. Pressure treated wood lasts longer than wood that has not been treated, but if you are ever planning on having your facility be organic, you might want to check with your local authorities, because some consider pressure treated wood to be a non-organic element. Also it is more poisonous to horses when they chew on it.

ELECTRIC

You can protect your fences from horses and horses from fences by placing an electric wire, preferably one strand above the fence and one at about (low to mid) shoulder height. Just know that electric fencing is high maintenance in that it needs to be checked regularly. If it is touching anything, it will ground the whole fence line, making it useless.

Some people even use electric fencing, 4-5 strands, as THE fencing material. It's an option. I'm just not as comfortable with this type of fencing as some others may be. I don't mind using it as re-enforcement on existing fencing, but am cautious about its use as a primary fence.

METAL PANELS

Overall, I like metal panels. They are versatile. You can move them and change the size and shapes of your paddocks. If and when horses kick them, they may bend or dent a bit, but they do not break, so you do not have to be too worried about two horses you really don't want in the same field accidentally getting together. One important note on metal panels is to go with a five rail panels. I have heard of horses strangling themselves in four rail panels.

HOG FENCING

Old-fashioned hog fencing is very common on a lot of established ranches. It's not all bad. It is often ok for perimeter fences in which there will be no horses on the other side of it. But, horses can step on it and occasionally get their hooves caught in it. While it is more unlikely for this to happen at outer edges of the property, this will be something that you need to consider. Some properties are too large to consider re-fencing, but a nice alternative is an electric wire on the top. I would not recommend it for any fencing that separates horses.

WIRE HORSE FENCING

An alternative to hog fencing is horse fencing, which is a 2"x4" wire mesh fencing material and is available in several heights. This is a popular style of fencing in many areas and can be topped with a wood corral board to minimize horses leaning over it and stretching it. The problems I have experienced with it are the horses rub against and break it down over time. So either you need a wood board at (mid to low) shoulder height or an electric wire to keep them from leaning against it. I highly recommend a top rail to keep the horses from leaning and rearing up onto it.

SEPTIC AND WELL SYSTEMS

Because horse properties tend to be in rural or country locations, you may need to educate and research the well and septic requirements of the facility you are looking at or planning to develop. Septic and well systems vary tremendously based on the geographic area and county requirements. So before purchasing an existing facility or ready to build, make sure to go to your local county planning department and find out what your requirements are. These systems can be either reasonable to install and repair or they can be wildly expensive.

Since you will be having the public at the facility you also want to make sure if the water is safe to drink and that you will be able to provide sufficient restroom facilities. You can take a sample of your water to a local lab and have it tested. You can also provide port-potties and bottled water if in doubt about your septic and well systems.

USE PERMITS

Since you will probably be going to your local planning department, also check on the parcel you are evaluating and find out what use permits it has and if it has any existing violations or limitations. Agricultural land is very different from city properties. There are all sorts of regulations that you might not be aware of, that you should know before committing to a property. Use permits vary from county to county, and if you are having trouble navigating this terrain on your own, find an experienced person who can help you. A realtor or staff person in your planning department might be able to recommend someone who can assist you.

FOLIAGE

What plants and trees are on the property? Check with your local veterinarian for toxic plants to avoid. Some of the most beautiful landscaping plants are also fatal if ingested by horses. Also if you will be working outside, is there shade for your customer(s) to sit under or do you need to provide umbrellas or other sources of shade?

MY STORY

When I bought the ranch in Valley Ford, California, it only had a house on it. There were no barns. The land was very wild in that for 10 to 20 miles surrounding the ranch in any location, land use was primarily grazing animals, which allowed a lot of open space for coyotes, mountain lions, bobcats, etc. The previous owner had built the house on the top of a treeless hill overlooking the neighboring valleys, which was beautiful indeed, but extremely prone to the elements. I decided to live on the land for a year before I built the barn to really feel the weather patterns. Because I knew from being in the area for many years, that the weather could be very extreme near the coast especially on top of an unforested mini-mountain. The terrain was extremely hilly with numerous, dramatic ravines carving the land. Stunning to view, but difficult to work with in terms of finding a place to set the barn and pastures.

My choices were limited to one particular area. A brief plateau in the midst of dramatic sloping grassland. Not my first choice. I would have preferred flat to gently rolling hills, to provide lots of small to large pasture areas for horses spanning off the main barn. But having grown up in the area, I knew horses do just fine in a wide variety of terrain. It's their human counterparts that usually are concerned.

I knew I wanted large pastures for horses to be herds together and to have plenty of grazing opportunity, and the land surely provided that. But something was missing. The butterflies and hummingbirds. Ladybugs and snails. Early in the morning and near dusk, I would often get the feeling of pain or hurt. It was hard to describe or to ascertain on an intellectual level. I would get the distinct impression that the land was wounded. To this day, I do not know its full history, except that a native band of Miwok Indians used to live in the valley below. What happened to them, I do not know. What I did know was that this top-of-the-hill was a powerful place of prayer. I offered to tend to it, to do my best to respect it and to nurture it back to health.

I planted lots of flowering plants, spread native seeds each spring. I took my time in deciding on the barn location. When it came time to build the barn, I knew the force and frequency of the spring winds off the coast coming from the west were the dominating weather factor. While winter storms were significant with their dramatically high winds coming from the south and occasionally from the North, the spring winds were more frequent and the main issue I decided to design the barn to compensate for. I did not want to cover all 4 sides of the arena, as I like an open feeling. I like to feel the breeze and see the horizon. But I also knew that the spring winds were prohibitive to doing EGE work and training horses.

So I designed the barn to run lengthwise from north to south so that the stalls would protect the arena from the spring winds. I knew that the winter storms would blow through the arena, but since it would be covered, it would protect the stalls and hay storage from the brunt of the storms. I fenced the arena with a combination of wood corral boards and panel fencing. The east side of the barn was fenced with metal panels since the pasture horses shared the same fence. The inner, east fencing of the arena I did in wood for the pleasing affect it has. For the barn itself, I used tongue and groove wood paneling and metal roofing. Between the arena and the 12'x12' stalls, runs a 12' breezeway which cars and trucks can drive through, horses can be easily walked through and even tied.

On the north end of the barn, I fenced 20' off of the 80'x180' arena to act as a pasture overhang so that the field horses could get out of the rain to eat and dry their feet. The accompanying field is approximately 30 acres of which I can fence off 25 acres when the grass gets too rich for the horses to be out on 24/7. Another 10 acre field lies to the west of the barn and has a 12'x24' pasture shelter open on 3 sides. On the south end of the barn there are 3 large paddocks that come off of the stalls. One paddock is approximately 2 acres and the other 2 are 1 acre each. In addition, a 24'x48' paddock and 50' round pen come directly off of the arena.

In effect, all of the horses in all of the pastures, stalls and paddocks can interact with each other and with the EGE process. The horses never feel isolated from each other even if they are not in the same field. The round pen juts out into the main pasture where an average of 10-20 horses reside and it is amazing how sometimes it is particular horses in the pasture herd who come along at just the right moment and offer their gift to the EGE process. The barn basically sits in the middle of the horses.

The round pen is made of pipe panels and is the first round pen I have ever utilized. I did not grow up with a round pen and so I do not use it for training horses. But it has proven to be a nice, round space for some of the EGE work. It has an open feeling and looks out onto some dramatic landscape. Its roundness and circle form can also create a nice metaphor for EGE work.

Grain bins were built out of wood and I built plenty to grow into. Same with the hay storage. I tried to plan for growth, which I almost immediately grew into. I have a place to park tractors too. I use a porta potty and pay for bottled water for human consumption. I even built in a 12'x 24' conference room that easily holds up to 20 people.

I miss having an outdoor arena, but you can't have it all. So there you go. And I am happy to report that the hummingbirds and butterflies are back. The raptors visit daily and live in and among the barn. The land seems peaceful now and contributes greatly to the EGE work.

CHOOSING HORSES

Choosing horses that are meant for this work takes finesse, experience and intuition. If you are not sure you are experienced enough to choose a horse on your own, hire someone who does (I can help you). It is worth the money spent. All horses are intuitive and sensate. All reflect our emotions and offer the required sensitivity to reveal the inner workings of the persons they are around. But, some horses are too sensitive. Some horses find unconfident people scary, because they are also unconfident. Some horses find incongruent people to be dangerous to their safety and they will become extremely aggressive in their attempt to save themselves. Some horses are too self-centered, thinking of their own self-preservation first and forgetting that humans are present. Some horses are too spooky. Even if they only spook once in a rare while, if they spook explosively and dramatically, they might not be well suited for this work.

Most horses will respond dramatically differently to youth than to adults. This is an important consideration. A horse that works great in a youth program may be irritated and too aggressive for adults. Horses tend to have more patience with young people.

Another consideration is that you might have a wonderful relationship with your horse, but that does not necessarily translate to other humans. Some horses hate men. Some horses hate women. Some horses are one-man horses and want you all to themselves. You also need to consider how you are going to feel when someone else is working with or handling your horse. Does it make you nervous, tense? If so, this horse may need to be your private companion, not to be shared with others.

Horses do not require special training to do EGE work. I prefer horses that have not been trained in specific operant conditioning methods, because sometimes they have lost their 'feel' or their independent thinking. However, horses that have been overly dominated or manipulated, can recover their senses if exposed to someone who honors and respects that they are more than tools or machines that need to be told what to do all the time.

Some rescue horses make the best horses. But, if you have a rescue horse, make sure you really know this horse and understand his history (not what someone told you, but rather your own observations of his trigger/fear buttons and how he deals with fear). Some horses have deep conditioned responses to very specific incidences. For example, I once had a little Hackney. She was a great lesson horse for kids. But every time the kids went to dismount, she would throw her head up, panic, try to bite you, the kid, anything. It's like she lost her senses. The only thing I could figure was that perhaps a previous child owner had fallen off of her often, and upon dusting him/herself off proceeded to beat her in the face with the reins. It was the only time she was ever head shy. But her head-throwing tantrum was dangerous to the little people's faces. Once I understood that she had a significant triggered traumatic memory, I was able to help her and the child to dismount safely. She never stopped having this automatic response. And I developed compassion for and acceptance of it.

Another amazing EGE horse, named Toyota, also had a traumatic history that I only learned about through the experience of being with him and witnessing his abrupt change in behavior. He was a dapple grey Arab with a large scar on his face. The woman who cared for him only knew that he had been beaten, but she did not know the details. 99% of the time he was a gentle, passionate, loving horse. He showed no outward signs of fear or trauma. He obviously felt safe in his current environment. We worked together four times a year for several days at a time doing EGE work with women leaders. It wasn't until several years of working together, that I finally saw his dark side.

A woman was in the round pen with him talking and he suddenly, and quite unexpectedly, started to run around the round pen. He became terrified, wild eyed and before I knew it he was starting to come towards the woman, threatening to attack her. This all happened in a blink of an eye-out of nowhere. Fortunately, I am a very seasoned horse trainer and read the signs immediately. I entered the space and tried to calm him down. He had lost contact with me, which was extremely unusual. My assistant waited on the outer edge of the round pen for him to stop briefly (which he did) so she grabbed a hold of his halter while I asked the woman to leave the round pen (for her safety). I was very worried about Toyota. He was panicked, wild with fright. He had lost his ground. It took over ten minutes to get him to calm down. He was an amazing teacher to me that day of the power that incongruent emotions can have on a horse and how fragile this process really is. Even if it only happens once in a thousand times, it's that one time you never want to happen. Fortunately, the woman was ok, but apparently she had tapped into some deep trauma that was influencing the space and she was trying to avoid and deny it.

Making a long story short, I will just say that now that I know this about Toyota, I am super focused on even the slightest shifts in his comfort level. I promised him I would never let this happen to him again and I needed him to give me some warning signs. Our agreement has worked well. But the lesson learned is, "when you don't know a horse's history it doesn't mean he doesn't have one." I knew this as a horse trainer, but I had not experienced such an extreme response from a horse from 'out of nowhere' (distinct from a response to some kind of pressure or training). Extremely subtle shifts caused by anything in the environment can trigger the horse. You might not notice. Sounds smell, etc. Until you have seen a horse's full expression, especially when feeling afraid and unsafe, you do not really know what he is fully capable of.

Some retired horses also make excellent EGE horses because they have a history of loving to work and be part of a team, they want to engage with people and be of service. Since EGE does not require ride-ability, these horses can be excellent. Plus, they seem to possess a wisdom that comes with their age and experience (makes sense when you think about it) and is reflected in their resilience with people. EGE horses do not have to be sound to ride since most, if not all EGE work, is done on the ground.

Below I offer a few qualities I look for in a horse that I am considering to work with. An easy-to-use template that you can practice when evaluating a horse follows this review. Note that when I am interviewing a horse for EGE work, I am looking at the horse from a horsemanship perspective as well so that I can get a sense of the horse's willingness to bond to me as the facilitator.

OVERVIEW OF WHAT I LOOK FOR IN A HORSE

KIND EYE

I am looking for a horse that has a 'kind eye'. The horse has expression and life in its eyes. It is not dull or disengaged when I am around it. This term goes way back through horsemanship. The ability to discern a kind eye' may come from experience, I'm not sure because I have been around horses most of my life. So if you are not sure, begin to practice looking at horses and their 'eye' and what it means to you. Obviously, a horse who is 'wide eyed', usually appears spooky or nervous. Sometimes horses just have a very dis-interested look in their eye or even a look of disdain. A horse with a 'kind eye' gives you a feeling of warmth and good feelings. It's easy to start a non-verbal dialogue with the horse.

INTEREST

It's important to me that the horse shows an interest in me and in its surroundings. It expresses an awareness and sensitivity to its environment. I do not want a horse that is too expressive about its surroundings to the point that it becomes flighty, spooky or unsure of itself. I also do not want a horse that is too resigned or depressed.

CURIOSITY

I want a horse that is interested in people and has a healthy sense of curiosity. At the same time, I do not want a horse that is too nosy.

GOOD BOUNDARIES

I want a horse that has good ground manners. I would avoid horses that are pushy or lack a healthy respect for your space. Once we begin an EGE process, this becomes increasingly important. During an EGE process we may not require that the horse maintain the same level of boundary and respect for personal space as we might when we have our horsemanship hat on, but we want the horse to have a history and current practice of being in respectful relation to the human in normal circumstances.

WANTS TO DO SOMETHING

I want a horse that wants to do something, to be part of something, and who likes to work. A horse with a good work ethic naturally likes to engage in activity and enjoys a feeling of satisfaction after a 'job well done'.

REFERS TO ME

I want a horse to refer to me for direction when I am actively working with it. When the horse is unsure of what to do or how to respond, I want the horse to want to connect with me as opposed to disengaging and resorting to making its own decisions. This is very important. Part of this has to do with the horse's nature and part of it has to do with how I establish myself as the direction setter (or lead mare). Since I know that I have the competency to establish myself with the horse, I am looking primarily at the horse's nature or predisposition to accept me as the authority (lead mare).

If a horse does not have a natural tendency towards this kind of partnership, but rather tends to 'to do his own thing', I would probably not consider this horse for EGE. One reason is these types of horses tend to be self-centered. They think of themselves first. If a situation were to arise that needed immediate attention or was potentially dangerous, a horse that operates on his own can add risk to the situation. On the other hand, if the horse has a good practice of looking for 'good decisions' from the human (you), you will be much more likely to relax the situation and reduce risk.

WANTS TO PARTNER

When I begin to work in hand with the horse, I am looking for a horse that wants to partner with me. Who wants to figure out what I am asking. I do not want a horse that becomes challenging, aggressive or overly resistant. I also do not want a horse that is so passive that it just goes along with anything.

CONFIDENCE

I prefer a horse that knows itself and has its own sense of self-esteem. Horses that do not have self-confidence tend to be skittish, scared, clingy, and/or spooky which could create dangerous and unexpected responses during an EGE process.

As far as age of a horse, I do not have rules about the minimum age of a horse. I know that NARHA has standards about how old a horse should be to work with the public. I think this is probably a good rule that can help reduce problems associated with incompetent or beginner horse handlers. It is a good safeguard, but not an essential rule.

PRACTICES TO DO WHEN EVALUATING HORSES

STEP 1

Quiet yourself and allow yourself to enter into another state of consciousness.

- Quiet your mind, no rational thoughts allowed just yet
- Feel your body-temperature, muscles relaxed, the breeze in the air
- Feel your feet on the ground
- Feel your vertical line
- Eyes are soft, you are not using them as my primary sensory filter
- Check your mood; are you open, flexible, inspired?

STEP 2

Notice the environment the horse is in.

- Is the environment quiet?
- Where does the horse live? In a stall, paddock or pasture?
- What is the horse's diet? Is it on hot feed?
- What is the tone of the humans at the facility?

STEP 3

Take an initial view of the horse at a distance.

- Does the horse have a 'kind eye'?
- Is his/her attitude openly expressive or is the horse dull?
- Is the horse relaxed in its environment?
- Is the horse interested in the activities of the barn or is it recessed into the background, perhaps ignoring or avoiding contact?
- Is the horse's energy freely expressed or is it bunched up because it is over confined or for lack of movement or exercise?

STEP 4

Approach the horse in its environment.

- How does the horse respond when you approach?
- Is it interested in you?
- Does it make contact right away or is it hesitant at first?
- Does it extend towards you in order to make contact?
- Does it turn away from you?
- As you get closer you ask it a question like, "Hey, who are you?" Or "How are you?" "What's up?"
- Does the horse fee like it can respond and talk to you?
- As you reach out to touch the horse what emotion does it express?
- What role does the horse play in the herd if it is in a pasture with other horses?

STEP 5

Take the horse out of its resting environment and begin to work in hand.

- How does the horse respond to pressure?
- Does the horse move easily off of subtle cues, like breath, energy, intention, or does it need tools to know what to do?
- If it is used to being tool/technique trained, you might take a bit of time here and see if it learns quickly to listen to your energy instead of its memorized cue-response.
- You might apply a bit more pressure, or ask a horse with a bit more intensity so that you can see how it responds. Does it try to figure out what you want or does it resort to resistance right away?
- If you think the horse might tend to become resistant easily, you might be a little less refined in how you ask it to move (i.e. apply more pressure than you usually would) so that you can see if it is patient, or gets irritated.

Remember, you are not training the horse in this session. That is not your focus. Your focus is to listen and learn about the horse, not to fix the horse, work with issues that come up, or prove your prowess to the horse or to the human observers. Your job, in this moment, is to evaluate the horse as a potential partner in the work you want to do. Do not be sentimental here.

SUMMARY

If you've made it this far and braved all of the intensity that this book brings up, proceed. Make your dreams come true. Find a way. Don't give up. Share your love with horses any way you can, even if it's for free. Share your love of horses even when you want to give up. Share your love of horses wherever you are, whenever you can. Horses are keys to our soul, to our connection to the great mystery of life. Don' forget. Help spread the message.

When you feel lost, talk to your horse. Listen to his/her message. Do the work. Be a student. Learn, grow change.

Happy Trails!

APPENDIX A
HISTORICAL OVERVIEW OF 'HORSE AS HEALER/TEACHER'

1970's
1970 – NARHA's first organizational meeting
1978 – Linda Tellington-Jones begins TTEAM formal system
1985 – Sally Swift's *Centered Riding* published
1987 – Tom Dorrance publishes *True Unity*.

1980's
1989 – Ariana Strozzi pioneers the integration of horses in self-development programs, and begins the first EGE programs called Leadership and Horses™. Her book, *Horse Sense for the Leader Within* is published in 2004

1990's
1990 – Barbara Rector implements EFP in Sierra Tucson and founds AIA in 1991
1992 – AHA (American Hippo Therapy Association)
1996 – EFMHA is granted section status by NARHA
1997 – Linda Kohanov starts Epona Equestrian Services, and publishes *Tao of Equus* in 2001
1998 – Gerhard and Karin Krebs found G&K HorseDream in Germany
1999 – EAGALA founded by Lynn Thomas and Greg Kerstens to promote EAP
1999 – Ariana Strozzi coins EGE (Equine Guided Education) and begins the EGE certification program.

2000's
2003 – Equine Guided Education Association (EGEA) founded
2004 – The European Association for Horse Assisted Education founded by Gerhard Krebs
2005 – First Annual International EGEA Conference!!!!

APPENDIX B
2005-SURVEY RESULTS

Surveys were distributed by an email request that went out to approximately 100 individuals. The survey was open from September 1 until November 1, 05.

WHAT DO YOU CALL YOUR WORK?							
EGE	EFP	HAE	EAL	EAP	EFL/eel	Therapeutic riding	Not sure
13	1	2	2	2	3	2	6
42%	3%	6.5%	6.5%	6.5%	9%	6.5%	20%

PROFESSIONAL EDUCATION	
% with MA or higher degree	70%
% with no college degree	13%
% that have a coaching certificate	32%
professional degrees relate directly to human education/development	61%

# OF YEARS PROFESSIONAL HAS BEEN IN EGE PROFESSION	
Less than 2 Years	42%
2-4 Yrs	32%
5-15 Yrs	20%
Over 15 years	6%

# OF DAYS PER YEAR PROFESSIONAL DOES EGE WORK		
	0-10 Days/Yr	40%
	11-50 Days/Yr	20%
	120 days to full time	40%

EGE WORK PROVIDES % OF OVERALL INCOME FOR PROFESSIONALS			
Primary source of income	30%		
This is not their primary source of income	70%	% of time professional does other work	
		25% is other work	6%
		50% or more is other work	68%
		75-100% is other work	35%

# OF YEARS EGE PROFESSIONAL HAS WORKED WITH HORSES			
1-5 yrs	46%	65% of professionals have worked with horses for 10 years or less	
6-10 yrs	19%		
11-15 yrs	13%		
16-25 years	3%		
25+ years	19%		

FACILITY AND HORSES	
Professionals that own their own property and horses	42%
Professionals that rent property and use their own horses	16%
Professionals that rent property and horses	42%

Ariana Strozzi

DEMOGRAPHICS OF CLIENTS/STUDENTS	
Adults only	58%
Adults 75% and Students 25%	6%
Adults 50% and Students 50%	20%
Youth Only	16%

Professional works with Individuals only-100% only	16%
Professional works Indiv. 50% and Groups 50%	26%
Professional works Indiv. 25% and Groups 75%	19%
Professional works with Groups 100% only	39%

SUMMARY OF 2005 SURVEY

This survey indicates that many of the professionals entering this field are well educated. 87% have a college degree or higher, 32% are certified coaches. It also indicates the majority of professionals coming into this field do not have a significant amount of horse experience. 65% have less than 10 years experience with horses. 46% have less than five years of horse experience.

For the majority of EGE professionals, EGE is not their primary source of income. 70% supplement their income with other work. 42% rent facility and horses. 16% rent facility and own their horses, while 42% own their horses and facility.

The fact that only 30% of the horse/human professionals are making a full time living could be caused by several factors. They might not want to do this work full time. They might not know how to market themselves effectively. They might not be doing good work, which would account for low referral of customers. In addition to these individualistic variables, I think that the scattering of acronyms, too numerous to memorize or keep track of, confuses the marketplace making it difficult for all of us to be as successful as we could be if we were unified under one title, (i.e. Nurse or chiropractor). Hopefully we will continue to address this as an industry and learn to unify so that we can all be more successful.

APPENDIX C
CODE OF ETHICS OF THE EQUINE GUIDED EDUCATOR

EQUINE GUIDED EDUCATOR ETHICS

- I will identify my level of competence to the best of my ability in conjunction with a teacher or mentor, and will not misrepresent my qualifications, expertise, or experience.

- I will engage the horse as a respected guide, as opposed to a tool or prop that is manipulated through activities.

- I will encourage the integration of mind, body and spirit during the equine-guided education experiences.

- I will offer participants grounded assessments/feedback regarding the horse's behavior and responses where appropriate.

- I will not coach or consult client(s) when I am under the influence, or the client is under the influence of alcohol or illegal drugs.

- I will maintain appropriate professional boundaries and will not engage in sexual relations with client(s) or client's spouse or partner, during the course of and for a minimum of three months after the educational process.

- I will not exploit my client(s) trust. I will not use my professional relationship with my client(s) to further my own interests, and will discuss with my client(s) any potential conflict of interest that may arise at the outset or during the education process.

- I will refer client(s) for other services beyond my own competence as determined by my education, training and experience (e.g. psychotherapy, business development, legal advice, etc.)

🐎 I have a responsibility to maintain confidentiality about my client(s) concerns, not revealing any information about my client(s) to other parties, except where permission is given.

🐎 My actions are aligned with the concerns of my clients.

RESPONSIBILITY TO MY COLLEAGUES AND TO EGE

🐎 I will treat colleagues with respect, courtesy, fairness, and good faith, and cooperate with colleagues in order to promote the welfare and best interests of the client.

🐎 I will respect the confidences of colleagues that are shared in the course of their professional relationships.

🐎 I will refrain from gossip and private conversations about colleagues.

🐎 When advertising I will accurately represent my competence, education, training, and experience relevant to my professional practice.

EQUINE GUIDED EDUCATOR STANDARDS

🐎 I will communicate clearly the terms and expectations of the education process. This will include what I promise to provide for the client and what I will not promise.

🐎 I will create a supportive learning environment for the authentic expression of ideas and feelings of my client(s).

🐎 I will dedicate appropriate time to educate participants in how to stay safe in the process of working with horses.

🐎 I will wear professional attire when working with client(s).

🐎 I will maintain professional standards of being on time for appointments and returning calls/emails in a timely fashion.

🐎 I will consult, associate, and collaborate with EGEA and other EGE professionals where beneficial to the client.

Ariana Strozzi

I will gain written permission from each client before releasing their names and contact information for reference purposes.

 I will take reasonable efforts to store, transfer and dispose of client records in ways that protect client confidentiality.

 I will not teach other professionals the Equine Guided Education process until I am deemed competent and certified to do so and must demonstrate that I have been a full-time EGE professional for over six years.

PROFESSIONAL COMPETENCE AND INTEGRITY

 I will maintain high standards of professional competence and integrity.

 I will seek appropriate consultation/education for my personal and professional development and supervision/mentorship when I am practicing new concepts.

 I will remain abreast of developments in my field. Specifically, I will keep abreast of the advancements in the field Equine Guided Education by taking a minimum of **sixteen hours per year of continuing education.**

RESPONSIBILITY TO EGEA

 I will maintain accountability to the ethics and standards of the Equine Guided Education Association.

 I will enhance the public understanding and promotion of Equine Guided Education as a powerful learning process.

 If a professional question or need for supervision arises, I will contact EGEA for resources, referral, and/or supervision.

 To maintain status as an Equine Guided Educator I will maintain my membership with the Equine Guided Education Association and will take a minimum of 16 hours of continuing education per year.

CONSEQUENCES OF UNETHICAL BEHAVIOR

In the event a client makes a complaint to EGEA regarding unethical behavior by a certified EGE the EGEA Review Board will research and review the complaint, producing a report on the matter. If the Review Board substantiates the complaint, and thereby deems an EGE to have engaged in unethical behavior or unprofessional conduct, that person may lose certification and endorsement by EGEA.

APPENDIX D
ACRONYMS

EGE-Equine Guided Education
EGC-Equine Guided Coaching
EGL-Equine Guided Learning
HGC-Horse Guided Coaching
HGE-Horse Guided Education
EAP-Equine Assisted Psychotherapy
EAL-Equine Assisted Learning
EALC-Equine Assisted Learning & Coaching
EAC- Equine Assisted Coaching
EAEL- Equine Assisted Experiential Learning
EALT- Equine Assisted Learning & Therapy
EAGLE- Equine Assisted Growth, Learning & Education
EAPD- Equine Assisted Personal Development
EAT- Equine Assisted Therapy
EAMH-Equine Assisted Mental Health
EAE-Equine Assisted Education
HAE- Horse Assisted Education
HAPD- Horse Assisted Personal Development
HAC- Equine Assisted Coaching
HAL-Horse Assisted Learning
EFP-Equine Facilitated Psychotherapy
EFL- Equine Facilitated Learning
EFC-Equine Facilitated Coaching
EFEL- Equine Facilitated Experiential Learning
EFMH-Equine Facilitated Mental Health
EFSA- Equine Facilitated Self Awareness
EEL-Equine Experiential Learning

EEEL-Equine Experiential Education & Learning
EEE-Equine Experiential Education
EELC-Equine Experiential Learning and Coaching

Epona
EIP-Epona Instructor Partners
EAI-Epona Approved Instructors

BIBLIOGRAPHY

Adizes, Ichak. *Corporate Life Cycles*. New Jersey: Prentice Hall,1988.

Collins, Jim. *Good to Great.*, New York: Harper Business, 2001.

Dorrance, Tom. *True Unity*. Idaho: Give it a Go Enterprises, 1987.

Gatto, John Taylor. *A Different Kind Of Teacher*.

Knapp, Shannon, with Brenda Damman. *Horse Sense, Business Sense*, 2007

Leider, Richard J. and Shapiro, David A. *Repacking Your Bags, Lighten Your Load for the Rest of Your Life*. San Francisco, Berrett Koehler, 2002.

Ries, Al and Laura. *The 22 Immutable Laws of Branding*, New York: Harper Business, 1998.

Sharpnack, Rayona, *Trade Up! 5 Steps to Redesigning Your Leadership and Life From the Inside Out*. San Francisco, Jossey Bass, 2007.

Swift, Sally. *Centered Riding*. Vermont: A Trafalgar Square Farm Book, 1985.

sba.gov.bplans.com

startupepa.org

microsoft.com/smallbusiness/startuptoolkit

myownbusiness.org

ABOUT ARIANA STROZZI

I grew up on the back of a horse on the coastal hills of Northern California. To this day, I enjoy sharing my love of animals, land and nature with anyone who crosses my path. My mission is to re-connect people to the natural world for the sake of saving the Great Mother Earth and her creations. I believe that time is of the essence. We need to take the reins in our own hands, form herds of like-minded people, share our dreams and stand tall in the face of adversity. We need to awaken our spiritual longing and inter-connectedness to all life and encourage possibility and hope in a time of uncertainty.

HOW INTUITIVE HORSEMANSHIP™ INFLUENCED EGE

My work training horse and rider in a variety of disciplines from the late 1960's to the present (winning champion awards in dressage, jumping, eventing, gymkhana, reining, and working cowhorse) influenced my realization that horses were listening to the inner workings of a person-the subtle forms of energy, intention and imagery that emanated from them. I have always been a student of the horse and always will be. During my earlier years as a horse trainer, I learned that each horse is a unique individual, just like people are. Some horses learn better with an english techinque while others learn better with a western technique. I have learned that it's impossible to create a 'rule book' of how to work with horses that applies to the various personalities of different breeds and their environmental circumstances. At each stable I worked there was an implied, "This is the way you do horses and if you don't do it this way you don't know anything about horses." Being a young person who wanted to know everything about horses, I stayed open and curious. I learned quickly that the masterful horsewomen and men were using different techniques and tools, but they were getting the same results.

I threw theory to the wind, and began to look at the universal principles that lay beneath the art of horsemanship. What were these masterful horse trainers doing behind their tools and beyond their terminology? I began to see energy and qualities of being present. I saw intention, focus, patient resolve, direction and right timing. They had developed an intuitive ability to know when to reward a horse and when to create heirarchal boundaries.

Over the years, working with english and western disciplines and different breeds, I learned that these qualities of presence were fundamental. The tools we use as equestrians are just extensions of ourselves and are really only necessary as a last resort. These tools can be easily misused if the equestrian is not responsible for what they are energetically asking of the horse. For example, many beginner equestrians ask the horse to go faster by kicking the side of their rib cage, and yet they are inadvertently pulling back on the reins. The horse becomes confused and irrated at the mixed cues of their rider and start to get tense and resist. If the rider is not being self-responsible he/she thinks there is something wrong with the horse. The more effective reflection is 'what is the rider doing that is causing the resistance'? 99% of the time a horse is not doing what a rider is asking, it is not the horse's fault, but rather what the rider is doing or not doing that is causing the conflict.

The most efficient way to become a better rider for the horse is to be honest, just like they are, and to be self-reflective. The horse is a mirror of our inner thoughts, beliefs and possiblities (or not). To be self-reflective is to open the sensate part of ourselves that is still an animal. As humans, this biological birth right is often rusty and uncared for. It is taught out of us at an early age, simply through ignorance.

Horses, like wild animals, have a very keen sense of intuition and an uncanny ability to sense what is not spoken. Because of this they can often see things about us that we may not even be aware of. They are great teachers for us in the domain of intuition and intention. I find that the most interesting and effective way to learn universal horsemanship principles is to become a student of the horse. Yes, learning this way sometimes takes longer than applying a whip (or carrot stick), but the equestrian learns a universal way of working with horses that they can apply to any horse in any situation. The equestrian learns to respect the horse as a somatic being, a unique mind/body/spirit.

Ariana Strozzi

ZOOLOGY AND ANIMAL BEHAVIOR

While I continued training horses, I added wildlife studies to the mix. I cherished my studies of animal behavior at UC Davis where I graduated with a degree in Zoology in 1984. I spent several years working with birds of prey at the UCD Raptor Center and other wildlife at the UC Davis Veterinary School and often managed animal and equine facilities simultaneously. I incorporated the use of physical therapy principles (my mom is a physical therapist) into the healing and recovery of birds of prey dramatically increasing their ability to be released back into the wild. And for several years after I college, I managed veterinarian offices, while continuing to train horses.

SOMATICS AND LEADERSHIP

By the age of 25, I was training horses and studying leadership. I held several offices with the Petaluma Business & Professional Women's Organization. I loved the study of leadership, but kept finding my notes relating back to horses. I began to see that training human leadership skills was much the same as the principles of training horses. I was so excited by this revelation, I knew I had to bring the magic of animal communication into the world of people. I had the animal skills, and leadership study, but I needed more people interaction skills. So I began studying human dynamics in the mid-1980's. I learned aikido, and Somatics from Richard Strozzi Heckler. Richard and I co-founded the Strozzi Institute specializing in developing leadership and mastery in 1994. I continued taking leadership and self-development programs and learned from innovative thinkers like Julio Olalla, Fernando Flores, Rayona Sharpnack, Bob Dunham, David Whyte, and Angeles Arrien. I became a Master Somatic Coach and developed the Somatic Coaching Program at the institute.

The seemingly separate worlds of horsemanship and self-mastery began to blend together and ultimately shifted my orientation from traditional horsemanship (in which we control the horse's behavior through a system of cues and orders), to seeing the horse as a sentient being who can actually 'guide' us into a deeper connection with ourselves and our whole lives. I had always experienced deep transformations and shifts in thought processes with the horses for myself. But I started to have a sense that I could bring that to people who might not even want to learn more about horses. So I started bringing people out to work with the horses, not to learn how to work or ride the horse, but to practice energy awareness and centering. It was then that I realized that the horses gave each person a truly unique experience that directly related to every other area of their life. And so began Leadership & Horses™in 1989.

To this day I have been very fortunate to put theory into action and have coached over 5000 individuals in EGE since 1990. My clients have come from all walks of life including vice presidents, students, mothers, coaches, therapists, managers, small business owners, entrepreneurs, and corporate executives. My corporate clients include UC Berkeley Haas School of Business, Nike, Visa Credit Card, Wells Fargo Bank, Proctor & Gamble, Hewlett-Packard, Agilent, Cisco, Institute for Women's Leadership, Apple Inc, Leadership USA, PSI Seminars, Enterprise Performance, Strozzi Institute and various women's groups.

I coined the term Equine Guided Education (EGE) in 1999. I am the author of the book, *"Horse Sense for the Leader Within,"* and the DVD, *"Intuitive Horsemanship™,"* as wells as essays in the books, *"Being Human at Work,"* and *"Horse Crazy."* I am currently working on two more books. I co-founded Strozzi Institute in 1994 and the Equine Guided Education Association in 2003 with the intention of furthering the human potential movement. I am adjunct faculty of Institute for Women's Leadership, a Board of Director of Sonoma County Farm Trails and 4H Leader.

In addition to my love of horses, I am an avid rancher, winemaker, artist, and mother of three amazing children.

www.SkyHorseRanch.com
www.EquineGuidedEducation.org

707-876-1908
Ariana@SkyHorseRanch.com